Reviews of earlier titles by Mary Jane Walker

★ ★ ★ ★ ★

'Highly Recommended'

"This person is courageous. To actually leave everything behind, pack up and go. At the same time, to be truthful, I envy her. I'm sure it took planning and skill. Most of all it took all these generous and thoughtful people to be there. At first, I thought this adventure was going to be tedious. Turns out it's different, fascinating and wonderful. This book shows all elements like where you visit, how are the people leading their lives, what is the food like, the hotels or hostels are they secure, is the staff friendly, are the people you meet honest. Overall, I enjoyed this author and am looking forward to reading her again."

Ross Knight, review of A Maverick Traveller, *initial Amazon Kindle edition, 2 February 2017*

D1211432

'An interesting read!'

"There are a lot of interesting things in New Zealand. Like Mary Jane, I also love to travel and one of my so-called "travel-goals" is New Zealand. I often heard from my friends who have been to the country about how great it is, how fresh the air is in there and how breathtakingly beautiful the country is. In this book, Mary Jane shares her first-hand experience in New Zealand that will surely inspire readers to dream and pursue that dream to see this country. For me, this book is a sort of travel guide. You will [have] a lot of ideas as to what to do whenever [you] get the chance to visit New Zealand. I had a great time reading this book. I felt that I was already travelling there but of course, I will visit the country for real."

Joo Yoo Rin, review of A Maverick New Zealand Way, *initial Amazon Kindle edition, 30 March 2017*

PILGRIM WAY

MARY JANE WALKER

Mary Jane Walker is a writer of historically well-informed travel memoirs that come with an autobiographical flavour. She has been described as a younger, female Bill Bryson, though with her own unique voice. *A Maverick Pilgrim Way* is the fourth book in a series of eight.

Though she was born in New Zealand, Mary Jane's father was Scottish. She grew up speaking Dundonian, the Dundee dialect, at home. With dual New Zealand and UK citizenship, Mary Jane has also enjoyed being a citizen of Europe: though perhaps not for much longer!

In this unique book, follow the winding ancient roads of pilgrims across the continent of Europe. The Camino de Europa or European Road, a vast mother-network of individual Caminos each with its own name, traverses across nations, mountains and frontiers.

Strap on your backpack and your walking boots and come along for the journey. Across Europe there are a maze of walks to begin, incredible discoveries to be made along the way, and adventures to be had.

The best-known route is the Camino de Santiago or St James Way with a symbolic scallop shell leading the pilgrim along. This Camino is made up of many individual routes itself, converging like the rays of the shell. Mary Jane hopes one day to complete it in its entirety, one pilgrim's way at a time. The author even climbs Mont Blanc, the highest mountain in Europe.

Instagram: @a_maverick_traveller
Twitter: @Mavericktravel0
Facebook: www.facebook.com/
amavericktraveller
Linkedin: Mary Jane Walker

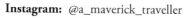

Other books by Mary Jane Walker

A Maverick Traveller

A Maverick Traveller is a funny, interesting adventure compilation of Mary Jane's adventures until 2016. Starting from her beginnings in travel it follows her through a life filled with travel and exploration of cultures, mountains, histories and more. Whether it was eating dog unintentionally in Indonesia, meeting the rapper 50 Cent at a backpackers' hostel or kicking a US nuclear submarine in New Zealand, A Maverick Traveller is filled with the unique stories and experiences of Mary Jane Walker.

http://a-maverick.com/books/a-maverick-traveller

A Maverick New Zealand Way

Discover the stunning back country of New Zealand. Come along with Mary Jane on over fifty walks and mountain ascents throughout the islands of New Zealand. Offering an interesting account of New Zealand history alongside tales of modern-day adventure, it is the perfect read to inspire you to get outdoors in New Zealand.

http://a-maverick.com/books/new-zealand-way

A Maverick Cuban Way

Trek with Mary Jane to Fidel's revolutionary hideout in the Sierra Maestra. See where the world nearly ended and the Bay of Pigs and have coffee looking at the American Guantánamo Base, all the while doing a salsa to the Buena Vista Social Club. Go to where Columbus first landed but don't expect to have wifi on your phone, only in hotspots using a card. People are proud and there's one doctor for every 150 people. Mary Jane loved it and did it.

http://a-maverick.com/books/cuban-way

A Maverick USA Way   *Release: September 2017*

Mary Jane took AMTRAK trains to East Glacier, West Glacier, Tetons, Estes and Yosemite national parks before the snow hit. She loved the Smithsonian museums and after seeing a live dance at the Native Museum, she decided to go to Standing Rock. It was a protest over land rights and drinking water, at 30 below zero! She loved Detroit which is going back to being a park, and Galveston and Birmingham, Alabama. She was there during the election and was not surprised Trump won. She was tired of being mistaken for being a homeless person because she had a back pack and left San Francisco because of it.

http://a-maverick.com/books/USA-way

A Maverick Himalayan Way   *Release: November 2017*

Mary Jane walked for ninety days and nights throughout the Himalayan region and Nepal, a part of the world loaded with adventures and discoveries of culture, the people, their religions and the beautiful landscapes. She visited the Hindu Kush in Pakistan and listened to the Dalai Lama in Sikkim, India. It is a journey of old and new. So, come trekking in the Himalayas with Mary Jane.

http://a-maverick.com/books/himalayan-way

A Maverick Inuit Way and the Vikings   *Release: December 2017*

Mary Jane's adventures in the Arctic take her dog sledding in Greenland, exploring glaciers and icebergs in Iceland, and meeting some interesting locals. She found herself stuck on a ship in the freezing Arctic Ocean amongst icebergs, and had her car windows almost blown out by gale force winds! Take a ride through the Arctic and its fascinating history.

http://a-maverick.com/books/inuit-way

Plus: *A Maverick Australian Way*, due out in January 2018

Published 2017 by Mary Jane Walker

A Maverick Traveller Ltd.

PO BOX 44 146, Point Chevalier, Auckland 1246, New Zealand

www.a-maverick.com

Email: maryjanewalker@a-maverick.com

ISBN-13: 978-0-473-40829-9

Disclaimer

This book is a travel memoir, not an outdoors guide. Although the author and publisher have made every effort to ensure that the information in this book was correct at the time of publication, the author and publisher do not assume and hereby disclaim any liability to any party for any loss, damage, or disruption caused by errors or omissions, whether such errors or omissions result from negligence, accident, or any other cause. Some names have also been changed to disguise and protect certain individuals.

Notes on Images

All maps have north at the top and have been drawn for this book by Chris Harris unless otherwise credited. The credit 'PCL' refers to the Perry-Castañeda map library of the University of Texas. All photographs in the book are the property of Mary Jane Walker unless otherwise credited.

Covers and Fonts

The front cover includes an image called 'A United Europe from Space', European Space Agency image ESA236276, CC-BY-SA 3.0, blended into the artwork. Front cover and spine fonts are League Gothic, rear cover fonts are Noteworthy (Bold). The interior text is typeset throughout in Adobe Garamond Pro.

Contents

MARY JANE WALKER

Introduction

T HIS book is about my journey across Europe and all the various walks that I have done to date on its pilgrim pathways. As befits an ancient cultural region, Europe is covered with a network of traditional pilgrim pathways. Many of these have fallen somewhat into disuse or been forgotten about among the general population; but are now being revived and popularised as hiking trails, even for those who are not especially religious. To follow such a pathway, trail, camino, or route – whatever you'd like to call it – is like doing a massive puzzle one piece at a time, connecting the dots and enjoying the adventures that each new country and pathway brings.

I am a dual passport holder with a New Zealand passport and a British passport. My family are from Scotland originally, and my home has been both in Europe and in New Zealand. In some respects, I felt very much like I was a visitor in New Zealand. I grew up with a strong sense of Scottish history and spoke Dundonian: the local dialect of Dundee, Scotland.

Family history is important to me and part of my reason for doing the Camino de Europa (a Spanish term for the ancient Ways of Europe) is to get closer to those family roots. My mother's side of the family have started researching the family tree which traces back to family from Spain, France, Ireland and more recently England and New Zealand. Her family name started out as 'Mangan' and ended up as 'May' in England.

*'Scottish women waulking wool and singing waulking songs
on the Isle of Skye.'*

This is a detail from an engraving by Moses Griffith which appears in Thomas
Pennant, *A Tour in Scotland* (1772). Source URL: http://www.marariley.net/
celtic/images/waulking.jpg . The entire image appears in a somewhat less
sharp form as Figure 3 in Anne Margaret McLeod, *The Idea of Antiquity in
Visual Images of the Highlands and Islands c. 1700-1880*, PhD thesis published
online, University of Glasgow, 2006. A high-quality copy of the entire image is
available from SCRAN.ac.uk, Scran ID: 000-000-014-795-C.

My father's side of the family is Scottish and their last name is Walker. The
name Walker is one of the oldest in Scotland and relates to the occupation
of 'walker' –the person whose job it was to thicken cloths and material by
walking on them.

There is supposedly a Walker clan, represented by at least three different
coats of arms and three different mottos. In reality, I fear that these are
latter-day fabrications by souvenir-sellers, as there is no official Walker clan

Western Europe, including the UK and Ireland

chief nor tartan. The much less romantic truth is that Walker is simply a proletarian occupational surname also found in England, and that many in my father's family were born and died in the Scottish urban poorhouses. And so, I grew up being influenced by the histories of the Scottish urban poor, who spoke the Scots dialect of English and not the Gaelic of the rural clans.

Several members of my father's family had emigrated to Hastings, starting with his brother in 1950, then my father, then another brother and their parents. Though I was born in New Zealand, we all spoke Dundonian, a sub-variety of Scots native to Dundee. But I never gave such roots much thought until I visited my relatives in Dundee in 1984 and found that they spoke Dundonian too!

I had made an effort in New Zealand to adapt and to immerse myself in the Māori culture, learning Māori when I was younger. I felt I could identify with the ideas of colonisation and the loss of culture as I felt, and still feel, that Scottish people had been victims of this as well.

Thinking about all these cultures and traditions eventually led me to the idea that hiking the many pilgrim pathways of Europe would let me really get down to ground level. I could mingle with the locals and I was sure I would meet a range of interesting people. I mean, you've got to be interesting if you're crazy enough to walk over hundreds, and sometimes thousands, of miles on an ancient pilgrimage, right?

Many of these pathways converge upon the Iberian Peninsula, a network generally known by its Spanish name the Camino de Europa, its principal destination the town of Santiago de Compostela in Spain's north-western province of Galicia, north of Portugal. I have visited Europe ten times and I have fallen completely in love with Spain and Portugal, so the fact that the pathways generally led in that direction was an added reason to explore them.

Partly also, I had become very unhappy with the social problems in New Zealand. The increased homelessness in New Zealand is a major escalating issue. Therefore, going to Europe was not only an exploration of the Camino Ways that lead to Spain and Portugal, but it was also an investigation of how local communities in Europe are surviving. I was to learn quite a bit. The political situation in Spain, in particular, is in rapid evolution. Podemos is a relatively new political movement in Spain founded by a

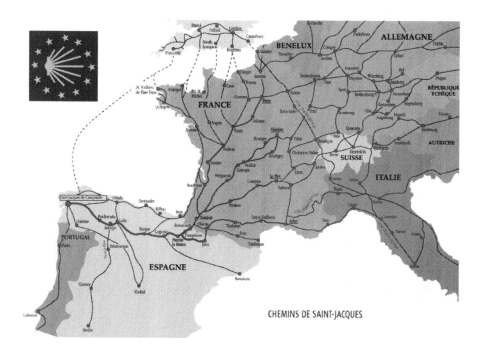

CHEMINS DE SAINT-JACQUES

The Camino de Santiago and some of its wider tributaries, with sea-shell symbol. The Camino has some British connections in addition to the Continental European ones. French translation by 'Kimdime69' of the German map by Mr Manfred Zentgraf, Wikimedia Commons, CC-BY-SA 2.5.

well-known Spanish political scientist, Pablo Iglesias. His aim is to address the unemployment, homelessness and inequality among the local people.

One thing I noticed in Spain was the acceptance of illegal migrants, especially the ones from South America. I was also amazed at the outpouring of compassion from the Spanish towards the Syrian and political refugees. I felt inspired by their views and how they were actively trying to help them in any way they could.

I also love the feeling of an interconnected urban community in Barcelona, the capital of Catalonia, the north-eastern region of Spain that some regard as a distinct country. During one of my visits to Barcelona the name Ada Colau caught my attention. In 2008, she formed a social activist group to address the situation of people being evicted from their homes due to the financial crisis in Spain. In 2015, Ms Colau was elected as Mayor of Barcelona and was the first women to hold this office. Her focus is on reducing the impact of tourism on Barcelona; she sees it as a cause of the destruction of local culture and wants to change that. Ada Colau is a different sort of leader, a leader voted in by a mobilised community to be mayor of Barcelona – completely different to local politics in New Zealand which is generally dominated by apathy and small turnouts. It made me admire her all the more.

Another place that was an amazing discovery for me was Portugal. It was an eye-opening experience, and to see a country do so well from its reliance on renewable energy was inspirational. I learnt that Portugal was 70% reliable on renewable energy sources – far more then Germany. Portugal was just a beautiful, hospitable country.

I decided that walking the pilgrim ways and climbing mountains was all part of my learning process. I had already trekked other parts of the world – the Himalayas, Nepal and Pakistan – but I had high hopes for the Camino de Europa. I felt it would give me some of the insight I felt I needed to understand the cultures of Europe as well as my own. It would be a journey which I wouldn't do in only two months, but would complete throughout my lifetime.

I was drawn to the companionship and the people I met who were from all walks of life. Many of the people I have met are still my friends to this day. I believe in fate and the mysterious workings of the universe that bring people into your path in life for whatever reason.

So, this is really an account of my journey so far along parts of the many pilgrim ways across Europe, with a few mountain-climbing experiences as well. There are walks everywhere – so many criss-crossing across Europe – and while I haven't done them all, I aim to do a part every year for the rest of my life. I have been lucky enough to experience so many different journeys, all of which I have written about, or intend to write books about.

Finally, while I have included many photographs, I have not tried to include isolated photographs of absolutely everything I saw or every place I went to. Rather, I have tried to include coherent sets of photos of the places where I spent most time. If anyone really wants to see what a place looks like in the simplest and most basic sense, they can look up pictures and videos of just about every place on earth on the Internet these days. Today, it is better for a writer to assemble coherent sets of photos that tell a story, that give a sense of the all-round feel of a place, or that illustrate a journey from start to finish. It is for such narrative purposes that most of my photographs have been selected, with the result that I have included several photographs each of some places where I spent more time, and none of others where I spent less time.

CHAPTER ONE

Who Were The Pilgrims?

I suppose any book about pilgrimage requires some background about it. This book is a collection of my different journeys, trails, routes, caminos or ways – whatever you wish to call them – all across Europe.

Europe's history, cultures and people are inextricably linked and the thousands of pilgrims that have done some, or all, of these walks all have a story to tell. Mine is but one in thousands.

First and foremost, I was raised (partly) in the Roman Catholic tradition, with which most of the pilgrim ways of Europe are connected, especially and for rather obvious reasons the ones that converge on Spain and Rome, as most of them do. My mother was brought up a Catholic, and when we were children she would take my brother, sister and I to mass every Sunday morning – rain or shine. My father on the other hand was raised in the Scottish Episcopal Church: staunchly Protestant. Quite literally, as a humorous old song has it, my father he was Orange and my mother she was Green.

Back then I was a self-confessed hippie and would wear off-the-shoulder dresses, flowers or headbands in my hair, and have string tied around my bare feet. That is how I would go to mass – much to the dismay and disdain of other church members. I would describe myself now as a lapsed Catholic; I don't go to mass, but I still have a deep-founding appreciation and respect for not just Catholicism, but all religions. I have prayed in many different types of houses of worship. I have attended a three-hour lecture on the

history of the Russian Orthodox Church, an outdoor sermon in the streets of Lourdes, and I have been to the island of Patmos to see remnants of St John the Apostle.

The meaning of 'maverick' is someone who doesn't follow the crowd. To me it's a symbol of being independent; a term and way of life I live by. It's in my blood, and I'm proud of it too. So, naturally, I thought a pilgrimage was right up my alley, even though it would span the length of my adult life.

Going on a pilgrimage was something I have always wanted to do, and coming from a family with a strong religious background meant it was something close to home for me. Most if not all of the pilgrimages around Europe are related to some branch of Christianity. Having said that, the three major monotheistic religions – Christianity, Judaism and Islam – all share similar stories and often similar beliefs, while showing stark contrasts as well.

One thing I learnt on all my travels is that people make pilgrimages for all different reasons and they don't have to be religious. I met people who were doing pilgrimages as part of training for other sports, to just get away from their lives, or to have a break from relationships for quiet reflection.

The medieval pilgrims would usually undertake pilgrimages as an act of penance – for forgiveness of their sins, however insignificant or wicked they might be. Back then the poor, the rich and royalty all went on some form of pilgrimage. What surprised me is where they came from: they walked from all over Europe. For some, that meant only walking to the next town. For others, it meant walking across oceans and through many countries. The three main destinations that the majority of pilgrims strived to reach were the Holy Land, which is to say, modern-day Israel/Palestine; Rome; and Santiago de Compostela in Spain.

Santiago de Compostela, and its Cathedral of Saint James, plays a pivotal role in all the caminos. Most of the modern-day caminos all end up in the same place: Santiago de Compostela. I have my eye on that as a final destination. I knew before I started that I wouldn't be able to do the entire route all at once. I am a random traveller and go where I feel I need to go. This book is really a record of all the walks I have done, and how they connect and link up with one another to become the mighty Camino de Europa.

You may be wondering why Santiago de Compostela is such a significant place. Why there? The history goes right back to very beginning of the first century when people were still figuring out Christianity. Officially, El Camino de Santiago, or the St James's Way, travels hundreds of kilometres from different starting points around Europe, all finally ending at the Santiago de Compostela Cathedral.

The St James's Way's importance lies with the Christian religion and with the fact that St James the Great, one of Jesus's apostles, is the patron saint of Spain. It is this figure to whom I shall refer, henceforth, whenever I mention St James, even though there are several other saints named James. The remains of this St James, the Great, are said to be buried in Santiago de Compostela in the north-western Spanish region of Galicia. The word Santiago means St James in the Galician language, which is closer to Portuguese than to Spanish even though Galicia is part of Spain; as does San Diego in the most official, Castilian, form of Spanish.

Galicians say Santiago, a name that has found its way to Chile, while Castilians say San Diego, a name that has found its way to California. However his name is spelt or pronounced, there are plenty of references to St James (the Great) in the Hispanic world, both the Old and the New.

11

The ultimate objective, in the form of the Cathedral of Santiago de Compostela. Photograph by 'Yearofthedragon', taken on or before 19 February 2006, Wikimedia Commons, CC-BY-2.5

The Iberian Peninsula, meaning modern-day Spain and Portugal were given to St James for him to go forth and spread the word of Christianity. But it is generally agreed that he never got there in life, because he was beheaded by King Herod Agrippa I of Judea and then turned into Christianity's first-ever martyr. King Herod is greatly disparaged in the Christian tradition and is said in the Bible to have died of being devoured by worms, a fate which Robert Graves interpreted in his *I, Claudius* as meaning maggots. Such was God's wrath.

Anyway, the story continues that after James was beheaded, his followers gathered up his body and placed it in a stone boat for his burial. They were all about to set off to bury James, when, lo and behold, a group of angels flew down from heaven and guided his body to its final resting place at the cathedral in Santiago. Amazing, right? Well, it doesn't end there. The location of his body was unknown to James' loyal followers until sometime in the ninth century when a hermit called Pelagius was wandering near some woods in Santiago, as it was not yet but was soon to become. Pelagius saw strange lights and noises and immediately went to the local bishop to tell him what he had seen. They went in search of the lights and found a tomb containing three bodies. One was St James and the other two were thought to be his loyal followers. It was Spanish King Alfonso II that ordered a chapel be built over St James' remains. This was followed by a church, and later the Cathedral of Santiago de Compostela was built as it is today.

Whether the story is true or not, people vote with their feet and millions have trodden thence along the many beaten and not so beaten tracks since the ninth century. Since then, other martyrs of Christianity and important people in Spain have also been buried in Santiago; a great honour for them and an extra enticement for the people wanting to head there.

The term used for Spanish pilgrims is *peregrino*. The peregrino became the source of a very profitable business; even back then the medieval people saw this and quickly set up shop. They built churches, metalled roads, bridges and settlements right on the path of the oncoming pilgrims. The purpose was to provide what the pilgrims needed: food, accommodation and water. This saw medieval towns and small settlements flourish, particularly on the Iberian Peninsula.

The iconic symbol representing the St James's way, the scallop shell, denotes a mollusc native to the Spanish coastline. The yellow shell on a blue background points pilgrims in the right direction. I saw the symbol painted on all sorts of things: tiles, sidewalks, signposts and trees. It was like having a little reassurance along the walk reminding you to keep on going! Going back in time, the medieval pilgrims would wear it on their clothing and it acted like a badge so people could see who they were and hopefully would offer some protection. The shell had practical uses, too, to hold water to drink along the way. Apparently, it was also used as a form of measurement for how much food or drink a church might give a pilgrim.

There are plenty of stories that explain why this particular shell is now the iconic symbol representing the Camino de Santiago besides the fact that it is native to the Spanish coast. Some say a knight covered in scallop shells brought St James' remains to Galicia (Spain). Other stories associate the scallop shell with the symbol of fertility. It also acts as a metaphor, with the lines representing all the different routes pilgrims can take to get to Santiago de Compostela. Travellers would collect the scallop shells at the beach in Fisterra at the end of their long journeys as mementos.

There are two other terms I need to briefly mention here as well: the Via Imperii and the Via Regia. The Camino de Europa, as I have explained before, is the grandmother of all caminos and is a combination of twists and turns, roads and ways, that eventually seem to all point towards Santiago de Compostela in Spain. The Via Imperii and Via Regia are a series of ancient Roman roads which make up part of the Camino de Europa. These imperial roads connect each country with a central common theme: religious sites. These sites form the basis of trails across Europe, from the Roman trading paths through the mountains around Mont Blanc in France to ancient trading routes through Eastern Europe. They are all one and the same, really, and I think the term Camino de Europa covers them all adequately.

Even before all this happened, Christianity was well underway in other countries and nations. There is a lot of debate about which was the first Christian nation, whether it was Ethiopia in Africa or Armenia in Eurasia. While the core religion represented in my book is Christianity, I don't want to alienate other religious groups and their pilgrimages. Many of the sites and countries I visited were also of religious significance to other religions that make pilgrimages a fundamental part of their practices: Jews, Muslims, Hindus, Buddhists, the Baha'i Faith, and more go on pilgrimages every year to sacred sites.

I believe that knowing the history behind each trail gives you more appreciation for them and a better understanding of the historical and religious importance behind each route. I believe that religion celebrates culture and traditions. I personally feel there is a spiritual force, but we must seek conciliation and have joint celebration between the religions.

My personal journey taught me a lot about the different people and places of Europe and how close, yet so far, they are. It taught me how all the places are connected by invisible lines and routes – the Camino de Europa.

So, come and travel down the paths of the caminos with me.

CHAPTER TWO

Greece and Turkey – The Cave of the Apocalypse

GREECE

The Islands of the Aegean north of Crete, including Patmos

First Olympic Games, 776 BCE	Early Greek Culture: Homer's *Iliad* and *Odyssey*, ca 750 BCE
Greeks defeat Persians at Battle of Marathon, 490 BCE	Rise of Athens, ca 450 BCE
Rise of Greek Theatre ca 440s BCE	Parthenon completed, 432 BCE
Peloponnesian Wars between Athens and Sparta, 431 to 404 BCE, ending in Spartan victory	Romans annex Greece, 146 BCE
Fall of Western Roman Empire, 476 CE, Eastern Empire 1453 CE. Ottoman Turkish domination of Greece thereafter.	
Greek War of Independence, 1821-1832	Modern Olympic Games, 1896
Dictatorship of the Colonels, 1967 to 1973	Joined Eurozone, 2001

Greece timeline

Before I made the move to England to take up the teaching job I describe in *A Maverick Traveller*, I visited Greece and was really disappointed with it all. Don't get me wrong – I love Greece. I love the people, the food, the ruins and the rest. But my trip there that time didn't go so well!

Greece was an unintentional part of my Camino de Europa travels, as I was invited there by a friend. I am glad that I did go, but I feel that my travels there weren't the best reflection on what Greece has to offer.

Greece was the epicentre for Christianity in Europe in Roman times. It was frequented by some of the twelve apostles, and Greece then became responsible for spreading the gospel through other parts of Europe and as far as Africa and Asia. The Greeks helped guide Christianity into Egypt as early as 33 CE — CE means Common Era, formerly known as AD, *Anno Domini*, Year of our Lord — although Christianity is today a minority religion there. Christians in Egypt mostly belong to the Coptic Orthodox Church, which is related to the Greek Orthodox Church.

A central figure in Greece's strong ties with Christianity was John the Apostle. He would have to be my favourite apostle. Why? I just think he was a really interesting character and achieved so much at a time when Christians were being persecuted and murdered simply because of their religion. It is thought that he wrote the Book of Revelations, which is part of the New Testament. I got to see where he wrote this book on the island of Patmos, off the Coast of Greece. Apparently, he was Jesus's cousin and in Patmos I learnt that John had set up five churches and spent time there preaching.

It's thought that John was sent to Patmos in exile when the Roman Empire was expanding and pushing Christians out, before the time of the first Christian Emperor, Constantine. Before Constantine, when Rome was pagan, the Christians weren't *always* fed to the lions: but it did happen from time to time. After Constantine adopted Christianity, the danger of persecution became a thing of the past.

John lived in a cave that has now become a tourist hot spot. It's called the Cave of the Apocalypse and you can see where he lived and wrote content for the Bible. Also on the island is an 11th-century monastery, which is also a popular reason for visitors to come to the island. The monastery is dedicated to St John the Apostle and you can see mediaeval artwork depicting him on the island. The island of Patmos is also part of the major Greek pilgrim walk called St Paul's Way, which heads to parts of Turkey, including Istanbul.

I had taken a ferry from the mainland specifically to see the cave. I felt blessed (I suppose that's the right word to use in this situation) to have seen it with my own eyes. My friend and I stayed in Patmos for three nights and I met many Greek Australians there as part of their pilgrimage.

Greece itself is a place that has meaning for Christian pilgrims and naturally there are many routes throughout Greece leading to many of the sacred places. These routes also interconnect with the Via Francigena, an ancient route from France to Rome. Greece is inundated with holy sites and shrines, much like neighbouring Italy, so there is no shortage of walks and routes to take.

TURKEY

Istanbul was a pleasant and welcome surprise. I loved everything about Turkey; the mixture of cultures and religions was just amazing. I was made to feel completely welcome here in a country so far from home. As soon as people found out that I was from New Zealand, they seemed to make a conscious effort to help me and talked to me about their friends and family who lived there. Turkey was nothing like what I had expected. My time

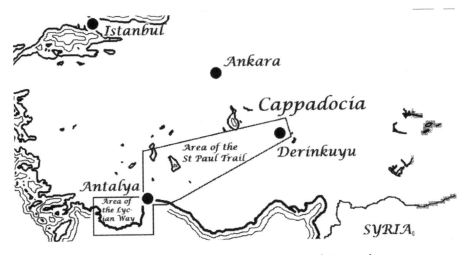

Turkey: The Lycian Way, St Paul Trail and Cappadocia

The ancestors of the Turks in terms of language and culture, were nomads in central Asia dubbed the 'Turkic' peoples. Some Turkic tribes migrated westward into the declining Eastern Roman Empire around 1000 CE and gradually took over the area of modern Turkey.

Modern Turks still remember the rich shamanistic legends of the original nomads, as do other Turkic peoples further east. Islam the main religion.

Constantinople, and last vestiges of Eastern Rome (also known as the Byzantine Empire), fall to the Turks in 1453 CE.

Turks expand their empire into Europe as far as the gates of Vienna (besieged in 1529 and again in 1683) but gradually retreat after 1683. Republic declared and new Latin alphabet introduced after WWI.

here wasn't very long (a meagre few days), but I really felt like I could spend longer here. Something that has played at the back of my mind since then has been to make another journey there, but for an extended period of time.

As I got off the bus, I was immediately swamped by the heat. I think that because I had sat on an air-conditioned bus for several hours, it took me a few minutes to adjust to it. The sky was cloudless and there wasn't the slightest breath of wind. It wasn't quite summertime, so it wasn't brutally hot – thank goodness. I headed off on a walk around the city as I needed to stretch my legs that had been crammed up against a bus seat for hours. I remember wandering around in the heart of Istanbul blinking with amazement! I was looking around and wondering where all the Islamic women in veils must be. Some women walked around with head covers and others didn't – I was amazed at how modern it was. Everyone was more than friendly and it wasn't culturally oppressive. Not at all.

In Turkey, the great majority of the population claim Islam as their religion. Islam places huge importance on pilgrimage as a fundamental part of religious practice, with their main pilgrimage to Mecca in Saudi Arabia. I find Turkey a really interesting place in terms of religious sites. It is a mixture of both Christian and Islamic sacred places. Islam adheres to the laws of the Holy Quran, which shares some of the same stories as the Christian Bible. I think that is why they are so tolerant of other religions in Turkey – in the same block there will be a church, a mosque and a synagogue. In fact, I saw a lot of tolerance of the Jewish religion too, which I thought was good. Turkey was one of the few countries that allowed Jews expelled by the Spanish Inquisition to come and live without persecution and to worship freely.

(When Queen Isabella of Castile and her husband King Ferdinand of Aragon led the Inquisition to remove all Jews from Spain, Turkey let them in and let them build their synagogues within their cities alongside churches and mosques. Incidentally, that is the origin of the term 'Spanish Inquisition'. What the Inquisition was set up to enquire into—the original object of its inquiry—was the question of whether someone who claimed to be a Christian was really a Moslem or a Jew; or, if such people were in hiding, where they were hiding. All the Moslems and Jews were to be discovered and expelled to the east: a foretaste of a later and still darker episode in history.)

The whole of Turkey is bursting with historical attractions and sites – you would not run out of places to visit any time! A treasure trove of pilgrim sites is scattered all over the country, including more modern ones such as the site of Gallipoli dedicated to the loss of New Zealand and Australian troops in WWI. There are plenty of connections to ancient Greece found in Turkey, which I was completely surprised at, though I shouldn't have been, because in those days what is now Turkey was in fact very much part of the Greek realm.

Like the English, the people who are called Turks today are the descendants of tribes who used to dwell on the fringes of the Roman Empire, and who progressively moved in as the Empire declined and fell. This decline and fall took until the year 1453 CE in the eastern Mediterranean: that is, the final fall of Constantinople to the Turks, after which the city gradually became known to the wider world as Istanbul. Thus, many of the architectural remains in Turkey are not only remnants of Greece but also of Rome: it really is something to marvel at!

Although generally thought of as revolving around Jerusalem and the Holy Land, the mediaeval Christian crusades were really aimed at preventing the Turks from moving into the vacuum created by the crumbling Eastern Roman or Byzantine Empire, which was centred on Constantinople somewhat further to the north, a city that was also the gateway to Europe. Ultimately unsuccessful, the crusades were attended by numerous massacres, persecutions, betrayals and acts of plunder and looting in areas through which crusader armies, passed from the Rhineland to the Middle East. All of this sowed the seeds of greater hostility for centuries to come. From that derives the deep ambiguity of the word 'crusade' in modern English, meaning something that is alleged to be a good idea in theory but liable to be disastrous in practice.

One of the major pilgrim walks I got to discover was the St Paul Trail, which travels through much of Turkey and is about a 500-km round trip. The St Paul Trail is said to follow one of the significant journeys the apostle Paul made through Turkey. There are several variations to the route, some sticking close to the Mediterranean port of Antalya where the St Paul Trail and another trail, the Lycian Way, converge. Other routes bring the pilgrims northward towards Istanbul where they can then (if they are really game) continue the pilgrim trail by connecting up to the ones in Greece at the Turkish border, and so on and so forth!

Again, sadly time constraints meant I didn't have time to actually walk the trail. The St Paul Trail is really popular. I remember sitting on one bus ride and looking out the window, snatching glances of a few weary-looking travellers with heavy backpacks and sticks wandering along the road. It made me itch to do it too, but I had to be realistic with myself – I had other commitments I had to attend to, such as work. For the seven days that had managed to set aside for this trip, I was going to make the most of it!

One of the first places I visited after Istanbul was Cappadocia, famous for one of the world's most iconic landscapes, which people often view from hot air balloons. Also near here is the underground city, Derinkuyu. Hidden completely beneath the ground, it is a maze of paths and rooms – enough to house 20,000 people. I was gobsmacked, to say the least. It was all hand built and just went on and on and on! It is most definitely something you need to see with your own eyes to grasp the actual scale of it. I walked down the narrow path that led down into the underground city and it took a few moments for my eyes to adjust.

The air was cool and damp down here with a heavy earthen smell. There were stone steps leading deep down into the earth, and the guide pointed out the huge stones that could be moved over the entrance way. What was incredible were the references to Greek churches depicted in pictures on the walls, and it made me wonder what they were doing there. I got my answer soon enough. The guide explained that in the past the inhabitants of the area had been mostly Greek. Because Cappadocia was often on the front line of the wars that raged between the Byzantine Empire and the Turks over several centuries, the locals formed the underground city into which they could retreat while armies passed overhead. I thought they were a resourceful group of people.

'A House in Cappadocia'.
Photograph by Brocken Inaglory, Wikimedia Commons, March 2006, CC-BY-SA 3.0

Turkey holds many important aspects for Christians: the Hagia Sophia, which was the biggest church in the world for many centuries; the fact that the term 'Christian' was first used in this region to describe the religion; and that the area that would later become Turkey was, of course, home to Constantine, the Roman Emperor who gave Christianity the boost it very much needed at the time.

After Cappadocia, I also did a few bus tours around the coastline down to Gallipoli and through a few other places. So, I did get to see some of the routes associated with the St Paul Trail: another connection to add to my Camino de Europa.

An approximate map of the Roman Empire at its greatest extent in 117 CE, not including vassal states and outlying cities associated with the empire.
After map by 'Tataryn' 28 May 2012, CC-BY-SA 3.0, 'Roman Empire', Wikipedia.

CHAPTER THREE

Ireland – Milking Cows and Finding My Way

IRELAND, with its rolling green hills and sheer cliff faces, is a myriad of historic and ancient sites. History is rich here. Religious battles, migrations, settlements, and churches hundreds of years old – it's all found here.

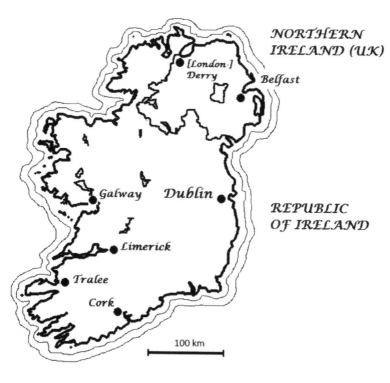

Ireland

27

Pilgrim trails in Ireland are becoming more popular and in 2016 they created an Irish Pilgrim Passport – a version of the Spanish one already in existence, where pilgrims collect stamps along the way and receive a certificate on completion. That's got me excited! Ireland's first National Pilgrims Day was held in 2014 and was aimed at reviving interest and knowledge about the ancient routes and paths all over the country. They have also started a National Pilgrim Paths Week held around April-May every year to raise awareness. I'd like to attend this one day! The most popular pilgrim trails in Ireland are the St Finbarr's Pilgrim Path, St Kevin's Way, Cosán na Naomh and Cnoc na dTobar. As with the Camino de Santiago, you purchase your passport for a small fee and get it stamped along the way. As this is a very recent idea, I haven't got my Irish version yet, but I do plan on obtaining one – maybe when I visit the recognition week! There are currently twelve nationally recognised pilgrim walks, though only five are included in the pilgrim passport. Some of these are the St Declan's Way in Tipperary, Brigid's Way in Kildare and the Rath/Dysert Pilgrim Path in Clare. Without even realising it at the time I had done some of these pilgrim trails around Tipperary when I stayed with friends there.

Ireland was settled during the Stone Age, so the walks around Ireland follow some interesting trails – ancient Viking trading routes and Irish saint trails. Irish history has mythical stories about the first settlers to Ireland. Ireland was supposedly invaded by six waves of peoples, the first being a woman, Cesair, who was a descendant of Noah, and the last being a group called the Sons of Mil from the Iberian Peninsula.

The majority of the people in Ireland are Christian. Catholicism is the main religion while in England it is Protestantism, and the battle between the two has been the source of many a war in Irish history. The evidence of these wars is still there today in the form of the great divide between Northern

Ireland and Southern Ireland. Northern Ireland is ruled by England and is closely aligned with Protestant rule. In fact, many of the Northern Irish people were English migrants who were gifted land in the 1600s simply because they were Protestant. Catholics were heavily persecuted in Ireland. They had land, property and even money taken from them unless they renounced their faith and became Protestant.

A group called the Irish Republican Brotherhood led a rebellion in Dublin while the focus was on World War I and a number of the leaders of the group were shot for treason in 1916. They were staunchly opposed to Irish involvement in the war and wanted to see a state independent from England. After the leaders were shot, the support for the group only grew, and it became the notorious Irish Republican Army (IRA, now known as the Old IRA). Today the successors of this movement, notably Sinn Fein, are still prominent in Irish politics with protests and movements for a unified, non-British-controlled Ireland. It is all quite sad and there is still evidence of anti-British sentiment in Ireland.

I was going to be spending time in Ireland and had decided I would try and see and do as much of it as I could. Ireland is actually a really small island, so it was easy enough to get around. The population of the Irish Republic is similar to New Zealand – around 4.6 million as of 2016 – with another 1.8 million in the North. My goal was to follow some of the main trails in Ireland. Climbing Mt Carrauntoohil was one and travelling to the most western point in Ireland would be another.

One thing I loved about Ireland was the people; they were just typical laid-back, welcoming people. The style of houses was so different from back home, though the countryside dotted with sheep reminded me so much of the countryside in New Zealand. Ireland has a lot to offer the avid history buff and also to those of us who love walking, hiking or just getting outdoors! No, the weather is not always the best, but I don't let the weather put me off or bother me.

Now, I have talked about the Camino de Santiago and the thousands of pilgrims who make the pilgrimage every year, but I'd like to draw attention to one connection that it has with Ireland. The Irish have a very strong DNA link to certain peoples of the Iberian Peninsula; as do the Welsh. Latest research into Irish ancestry traces the strongest connection to the Basque country in the North of Spain, which is also part of the Camino de Santiago.

This might be due to the existence, in prehistoric times, of some kind of coastal trading system: of settlement up and down a coastal line that ran from northern Spain to Wales and Ireland, by some seafaring people that might even have been the ancestors of the modern Basques, though languages related to Basque died out elsewhere. If we go back far enough in time, the Straits of Dover and much of the English Channel were dry land, through which the Rhine flowed southward, until about eight or nine thousand years ago. The coastal route between northern Iberia, Wales and Ireland would in fact have been fairly short and direct in those days, so perhaps that is the period we are talking about.

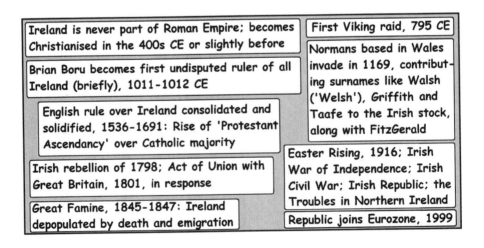

Ireland is never part of Roman Empire; becomes Christianised in the 400s CE or slightly before

Brian Boru becomes first undisputed ruler of all Ireland (briefly), 1011-1012 CE

English rule over Ireland consolidated and solidified, 1536-1691: Rise of 'Protestant Ascendancy' over Catholic majority

Irish rebellion of 1798: Act of Union with Great Britain, 1801, in response

Great Famine, 1845-1847: Ireland depopulated by death and emigration

First Viking raid, 795 CE

Normans based in Wales invade in 1169, contributing surnames like Walsh ('Welsh'), Griffith and Taafe to the Irish stock, along with FitzGerald

Easter Rising, 1916: Irish War of Independence; Irish Civil War; Irish Republic; the Troubles in Northern Ireland

Republic joins Eurozone, 1999

I had set out to begin a pilgrimage around Europe and that means walking a lot, but I hadn't exactly planned the moment I was going to actually start walking. I really felt I had to learn about each place I visited. For the first part of my journey I just explored by any means I could. This ended up being mostly hitch-hiking around, which was still fairly safe then, in the 1990s. I think I was saving up my big walk for the Spanish Camino de Santiago, much later on in the 2010s.

INA AND JOHN

I arrived in Ireland in the summer of 1996, a year after I met Ina in Ubud, the main city in Bali. She was travelling apart from her fiancé, John. We had got on well and so decided to hang out and sightsee together in Bali, at the time.

And so, I took a bus from the airport to Newcastle West, the town where Ina and John lived. Ina was a very strong-willed lady from Germany, and John was just your typical laid-back Irish lad. John was a farmer and had a small plot of land with a herd of forty dairy cows, and that was my first introduction to my pilgrimage, in a way – milking cows. How fitting, I thought.

John had spent some time in Christchurch, New Zealand, studying dairy farming. He was surprised by how big the herds were in New Zealand compared to Ireland. He also commented about how similar the landscape around Christchurch was to Ireland. Ina was trying to find work as a German language teacher. She had worked as a teacher in Germany. Ina had moved to Ireland and qualified as a teacher there, as she found Germany too modern and industrialised, then had met John and decided to stay. Ina described Ireland as 'old-fashioned', and that's why she loved it. It had this

31

Ina and I in Ubud, Bali, in the nineties

backward nature of things. Ina and John had only just got engaged, and were organising a party to celebrate their engagement at Ina's house in Tipperary.

Most young people who get engaged in Ireland tend to have an engagement party in a café. Basically, guests paid for their own food, while

Ina, John and me

the alcohol was provided on a tab. So, it wasn't one huge booze up and was a more civilised situation than I was used to back in New Zealand. That's what I liked about Ireland: they were genuinely laid back.

Ina was quite a spiritual person and she had organised for her and I to go to a retreat on the Beara Peninsula in the south-west of Ireland. It was a Buddhist retreat and I really enjoyed it because I do feel I have an affinity with Buddhism. About an hour into the lesson, the man who was taking the retreat (who just so happened to be an ex-Catholic priest) made a mention of heaven and hell. I couldn't help myself and burst out laughing. I didn't see any relevance of heaven and hell to Buddhism. Glancing over at Ina and her friends, I realised I had embarrassed them all. Still, I couldn't see it.

We also did the Millstreet Music Fair in Cork – only because Van Morrison was playing. I like Van Morrison, and to see him live was just such a blessing. I'm glad we went, as I really enjoyed it.

John had an aunt who had been a nun and also lived with him on the family farm. I learnt that it was an Irish tradition and totally normal for people to look after their aunt or uncle if they didn't have children of their own. They would move into a family member's home. I remember that Ina wanted the aunt to move out, but John wasn't going to let that happen. Instead, they decided to build their own house on the farm and were starting construction on it soon. I think that because the aunt was John's mother's sister, she was like a mother figure to him.

I went out with John and Ina to one of the pubs in Newcastle West. John joked around a lot and he very loudly informed his friends that we were getting married soon. I was highly embarrassed because every single man in that pub came up and kissed me, which John knew perfectly well would happen. That was not funny, I assure you! I did like the Irish people, though; they were charming and always liked a good joke!

DUBLIN

In Dublin, I did a loop trip on a boat around Dublin harbour, and loved travelling by water along the Irish coastline. I imagined how it would have looked to the Vikings coming to Ireland on their ships and being faced with the rugged coastlines. There is a church in Dublin known as the Christ Church Cathedral which sits looking out to the old Viking settlement called Wood Quay. Recent discoveries show that the church was actually built on the remains of an ancient Viking church. The original cathedral was thought to have been built around the time of an Irish-Viking king by the name of Sigtrygg II 'Silkbeard' Olafsson who ruled the area in the early decades of the eleventh century. It is believed he ordered the construction of this cathedral after his pilgrimage to Rome in 1028 – another link to pilgrimages right here in Dublin!

Another church I visited lay within an ancient Viking settlement, the only one near Dublin to actually be within the walls of a Viking town. The church of St Martin of Tours was a significant place to visit for many Irish pilgrims on their way to the Santiago de Compostela. Apparently, St Martin, who was born in Pannonia (now Hungary), began his early life as a soldier in the Roman army. He decided to leave the Roman army because it didn't fit his Christian beliefs and then pursued a line of work in religion. Martin eventually became the Bishop of Tours and his work saw him declared a saint.

I saw one of the oldest streets in Dublin, Fishamble Street, which was also established by Vikings. I was surprised to see so many visible links to the Vikings and how Christianity penetrated Norse culture in Dublin. I found it all completely fascinating.

Irish history was really evident, especially in religious terms, as wars between Protestants and Catholics marked much of the later part of Irish history. I felt I owed it to not only the countries I was travelling to, but also to myself to get to know as much as I could. I did end up learning a lot about Ireland.

You can easily see the importance of Catholicism and religion in Ireland through the many saints and pilgrim trails. To look out over Ireland with the rolling landscapes and the laid-back people, it is hard to believe that Ireland has had such a turbulent and violent history. I have heard the terms 'Celts' and 'Celtic' thrown around a bit to describe Irish and Scottish people. Another correct term for the Irish would be the Gaels; the Celts were people in Europe, of whom the Gaels – the Irish and the Scottish Highlanders, themselves of Irish descent – are a sub-group. At some point the Celts made their way to the British Isles in groups and settled there around 500 BC. Genetic studies have also compared Gaelic (traditional Irish) surnames with DNA results. They found that people with Gaelic surnames were the ones who generally had the same DNA as the Northern Spanish (Basque) Country.

What I really did like about Ireland was that all around the country you would see crosses. Just plonked in the middle of fields, all around, stood all these Gaelic crosses. You could even see ancient tombstones located everywhere; it was truly amazing. There, for yourself and everyone else to see, the richness of Ireland's history and past. The Gaelic crosses are a strong cultural and religious symbol for the Irish. In Irish, they call it the 'Cros Cheilteach' or Celtic Cross. Gaelic or Celtic crosses, like others, were originally created for religious purposes. They were either plain or richly decorated, each distinguishable by the inner circle that connects all the lines in the middle. There is one belief that the cross was created by the Irish patron saint, St Patrick, and it became a public monument in the medieval era. Some even claim it dates back to the time of the Druids. 'Druid' was a broad term used to describe the upper classes of the Celtic peoples around the time of the Roman Empire. Druids were usually educated and included occupations such as philosophers and doctors. Evidence of Druids has been found in Britain, France and even Spain. It is believed the Druids may have created some of the pathways in mainland Europe that were later to become part of the Camino de Europa trails.

GALWAY AND THE ARAN ISLANDS

I hitchhiked to Galway, a city lying in the west of the country. It is the third most populous city and bears the nickname 'The City of Tribes' after the fourteen merchant families who dominated the city for centuries. It sits within a county strewn with medieval Irish heritage and historical sites, and the climate here is just as changeable as your clothes!

Galway was a vivid experience for me – truly eye opening. It is a quaint coastal city with lush meadows bordered by low-lying stone walls, thick forests and castle ruins. I loved the colourful pops of colour on the buildings and the signs written in a traditional Gaelic style! I spent some time wandering along the harbour's edge, breathing in the salty air of the Atlantic Ocean. It was here I heard of the nearby Aran Islands and knew that I just had to go there. The Aran Islands hold a special place in the hearts of the Irish. Aran was once a place where people travelled to bury their loved ones in unique Irish cultural rituals. Aran's historical and spiritual importance lies, additionally, in the many ruins around the islands, including monasteries and churches. It was another significant part of the pilgrim trails throughout Ireland.

Galway is also near the iconic Cliffs of Moher in County Clare, stunning jagged cliffs stretching for eight kilometres along the coast that drops away into the Atlantic Ocean. The highest of these cliffs are at Hag's Head at 214 metres, and honestly, if you ever go to Galway or Clare, go and have a look. I thought it was quite amusing coming across many referrals to 'hags' in Ireland. I imagined all these old witch-like women with boils and warts running around medieval Ireland – I don't know. Maybe there was!

I don't know what persuaded me to actually go and visit the Aran Islands at the time, but I'm glad I did. I had heard other travellers talk about them and they seemed to be a popular holiday destination for tourists. One thing

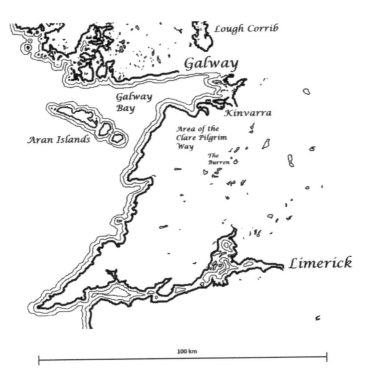

The area from Galway to Limerick, including the Burren

Galway, opposite the Aran Islands

Galway and its waterfront

I did learn while I was booking my tickets for the ferry was that 'ara' in Irish means kidney – so it literally means 'kidney-shaped islands'. Nothing intriguing about that name really… Collectively there are three islands that make the Aran Islands, or in Irisih, *Oileáin Árann*. The first people to the islands arrived 6,000 years ago, with the population growing steadily during the Cromwellian conquest of Ireland in the mid-17th century. The ancient Gaelic language, traditions and culture are still in use strongly here, which is why I have given emphasis to Gaelic placenames in this section, and the islanders have become the focus of enquiries made by anthropologists.

I caught a ferry from Rossaveel (*Ros a' Mhíl* in Irish), a port town in Galway, and within an hour I was on Inishmore (*Inis Mór*, 'Big Island'), the biggest of the three main islands of Aran.

There was a slight breeze blowing across the water as the ferry plunged through the waves. The sky was overcast, but the sun was brave enough to peep through every now and then. I generally found that the Irish climate was really mild, particularly compared to Scotland. I always expect rain and if it's sunny that is just a bonus. I don't get seasick very often, but I felt the bumps over the water a bit more then I had thought. The Aran Islands rose up out of the Atlantic Ocean and were much bigger than I had expected. We landed on a rocky stretch of shoreline on Inishmore and scrambled onto the rocky wharf – it really was just rocks. I remember getting off and the wind whipped around my head, a sheep bleated in the distance and we all scrambled across the shoreline and up into the grassy fields.

When I got off the boat and grabbed a little information leaflet off a stand. I remembered suddenly what had really piqued my interest in Aran, out of all the travellers' tales – the wedge tombs! Wedge tombs are a key feature of the islands. A wedge tomb is a sort of mini-Stonehenge with a sloping roof (whence, 'wedge') that also resembles a four-poster bed in

Aran Islands

some respects. Thus, a common Gaelic name for them is 'Leaba Dhiarmada agus Gráinne' or the bed of Diarmaid and Gráinne, a reference to two mythological lovers who supposedly slept in them in the course of travels around Ireland: this is one of a number of traditional stories and myths surrounding their construction. The tombs, around five hundred of them, are found all over Ireland, although mostly in the west and north of the country. The tomb on Inishmore was built in 2,500 BC, making it one of the oldest ones in Ireland, so yes; of course, I had to see it when I was in Ireland!

About 750 residents reside on the Aran Islands and almost 300 of them on Inishmore – while the towns aren't huge, they are a lot bigger than I had expected. They have restaurants and a few places for accommodation. The main town area is called Kilronan (Cill Rónáin) with a smattering of about 100 or so houses. There are some really neat accommodation places too– all stone and quite small, but homely and comfortable at the same time.

Two pages from a tourist leaflet I picked up on my first visit to the Aran Islands. (Out-of-date telephone number removed)

There are a few walks on Inishmore which just loop around the island and aren't difficult. I found them quite tranquil. I felt completely relaxed wandering around the island, and the day I went I suppose could be described as an off-season day. Yes, there were tourists and other people, but few enough that they didn't get in your way. The paths in some areas around the island were framed by walls of rock and stone. I found myself at a 15th century church with an old well that a few people were gathered around. Apparently, the old well's water has healing properties, but only if you truly need it and there was quite a strict ritual to follow about which way to stir the water, or something. I didn't have any but I watched in amusement as a few others had a go. Outside the front of the church was an area they called 'the beds of four saints' and since the church was dedicated to four of them I figured that they must be their grave sites.

All over the island are historical points of interest, including St Enda's monastery, which incredibly claims that over 120 saints are buried within the grounds. I was quite impressed with the state the monastery was in considering it was built in the ninth century. It was framed by a graveyard with rows and rows of Gaelic crosses. The foundation and core structure of the main house is still intact, and all the stones and some of the carvings could still be made out on the altar. The saint who apparently built it – St Enda – sounded like someone I'd like to meet. He was an Irish saint of the Roman Catholic Church, but on top of that he was a fearsome warrior king! I remember reading that information, and I thought, 'Wow, he would have been an interesting character!'

All along my walk I was stumbling on more and more ruins – I hadn't really known what to expect when I got to Inishmore as, originally, I went just to see the wedge tombs. I ended up to my eyeballs in ancient ruins and historical sites – a wonderful icing on the cake for my trip! There were churches, old houses and even a small museum filled with more wonders of the Aran Islands history.

I followed the trail to the beach and there was a huge rock structure sitting on the shoreline. It turned out that it was some kind of farming method where they were putting seaweed on top of the rocks and turning it into pasture. The term they use for this method is 'lazy bed' and it is often used to grow potatoes (of course). The island also had many beautiful little yellow flowers everywhere, prickly bushes full of them. They were furze, which is known as gorse in New Zealand. I thought that was incredible, because in New Zealand gorse is a weed that farmers and councils are forever trying to eradicate. In fact, gorse has long been seen as a useful shade plant for young trees and as an ingredient for herbal potions. Gorse flowers can also be made into a flavoursome wine, a practice that dates back to the ancient Celts. Of course, in New Zealand many of these imported species grow in a way that is out of control, whereas in their native habitat they are kept in check.

LIMERICK TO TRALEE AND THE BLASKET ISLANDS

The next Irish archipelago I would visit was the Blasket Islands, another historical part of Ireland I had always wanted to see. They are the most western part of Ireland and are a stunning example of raw Irish beauty.

While I was staying with Ina and John once more, some years after my first trip to Ireland, we decided to visit the Blaskets together. It was the summer once more and it had been unusually warm weather that year. After hiking a section of the Southern Trail, another attractive walking route in this area, we drove from Newcastle West to the little harbour settlement of Dingle. From there we took a ferry over to the Great Blasket Island (the main island of the group). It was quite windy that day and the ride over was quite bumpy, but the scenery all but made up for that!

The Blasket Islands, or Na Blascaodaí in Irish, are a group of six islands situated near the south-western tip of Ireland. The population was only ever as high as 175, and sadly everybody left in 1953 because by then they couldn't make a living. The government apparently made all the people leave by stopping all services to the islanders. In earlier times the islanders had done well for themselves and had avoided the Irish potato famine of 1845–1852. So, now it is just an abandoned island with a cultural centre for tourists and no permanent residents.

This part of the pilgrim trail through the Blasket Islands was important as part of the Monastic pilgrimages. It was a place of importance for pilgrims as well as Irish because of its strong sense of Catholicism.

John, Ina, Sophie (their daughter) and I were going to stay one night on the island in a modest, beautiful, old wooden Irish house that had been abandoned but then restored. There were many desolate houses and buildings around the island which had been left by families who had to

Ireland's Southern Trail. The solid lines are complete, the dashed lines are projected.

move to the mainland for work. Most of the walls and exteriors of the houses are worn away, but you could see that they were once beautiful stone buildings. As you approach the rocky shore, you can see that the homes were all built so that they all had ocean views, like steps down the sides of the hills. There were indents in the grassy hillside where you could see where the roads once were. There were a few sheep scattered around the island still, grazing lazily, unperturbed by visitors. The remains of stone walls peek through the grass layers that have started to grow over them. It was unusually warm there so we got to spend a lot of time outside doing the walks that spread out over the islands.

The Blasket Islands are stunning, and are quite hilly, which surprised me a little. The wind was a bit cold the first day and as I was so used to dressing in the New Zealand hiking style, I tucked the bottoms of my trousers into my socks and wore a woolly hat. Ina and John thought that I looked pretty funny.

CARRAUNTOOHIL

I'd often thought about climbing the highest mountain peak in Ireland; Carrauntoohil (Corrán Tuathail) is apparently one of the best hikes to do in the country and is located in the Macgillycuddy's Reeks, a mountain range in County Kerry. At 1,038 metres high it wasn't going to be as taxing as some of the other climbs I'd done. The walk we were going to do was a total distance of fourteen kilometres and an ascent of nine hundred metres. The area around the mountain has a long history, and quite a few artefacts have been found, including firearms that were probably used in the Irish Civil War of the 1920s. It was going to take around five to six hours to reach the summit and back. Ina and John's daughter, Sophie, was going to come with

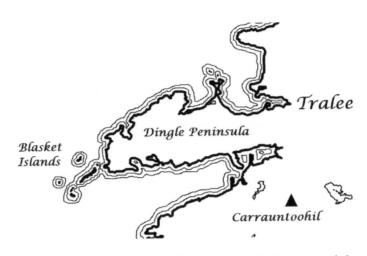

The Dingle Peninsula, Blasket Islands and Carrauntoohil

us, and we decided that going with a guide through a company called Kerry Climbing would be the best idea.

The guide gave us a leaflet that would describe our walk up Carrauntoohil. We started from Cronin's Yard, and I was feeling really excited.

In the twelfth and thirteenth centuries, Ireland was cleared of much of its forest, so there wasn't a lot of original woodland left on Carrauntoohil. Still, the scenery was great. There were about ten other people in our group as well as the guide.

We walked along a pathway that was two hundred years old – it has been the main starting point to the summit of Carrauntoohil for that long! It was a dirt track that slowly inclined upwards, wrapping itself around the side of the mountain. We came across one guy out taking his dog for a walk along part of it. I was surprised to find out that a lot of the trekking up Carrauntoohil was through private land. I panicked, and thought, 'Oh my goodness, we'll be barred access'. I didn't want to go all that way and not be able to climb the majestic mountain, but we weren't barred and so up we went. The landscape really reminded me of New Zealand.

Great Southern Trail

The Great Southern Trail

Old Stonework along the Southern Trail

John, Sophie and Ina and our trip to the Blasket Islands

Blasket Islands with old houses and panoramic view

Great Basket Island with abandoned houses, guest houses, and Dunmore Head

Great Blasket Island Shore

Blasket Scenes

Having a guide was great, as he pointed out things I might have otherwise missed. We crossed a small river shortly after beginning, then after about an hour of walking we reached Hag's Glen, and then it was quite a steep scramble among boulders before we got to the glen. It was a pretty setting; a small patch of flat land nestled between the rugged Reeks. Although a bit colder than I had expected, it was a sight to behold. Hag's Glen is named after an old folk story of an old woman who resided on the slopes at the bottom of the mountain.

She was wise, and people would seek her out for spiritual or medical advice.

There was a captivating arrangement of pinnacle-shaped rocks on the higher slopes. The trail continued to weave through rocky areas and through narrow ridges with sharp drops to the sides. I'm not really scared of heights, but Sophie, like I'm sure most kids at twelve, found it a little frightening at times.

There was plenty of scrambling among loose rocks as we made our way up the now very rocky track. We stopped for a break and had something quick to eat in an area that was used for rock climbing and were rewarded with scenic views. The ranges laid out like a crumpled blanket before us and seemed quite bare and barren – giant rocky hills covered in smatterings of grass here and there. I wasn't feeling tired by then; I was still quite pumped and excited to reach the top.

The next stretch of path was slightly harder, with huge stone slabs for steps that you had to really stretch to reach, and I felt my legs start to ache a bit. The group wasn't going full throttle up the mountain, but was taking it quite casually – which made climbing the mountain a whole lot easier too!

We continued on and passed by a small lake – I wondered how many people had wandered up here just to enjoy the peace and quiet.

The next part of the walk was not peaceful or quiet. The loose stones and pebbles slid under everyone's feet and started a small avalanche of small stones down the path after each step. This part of the climb was taxing – I'll admit it! O'Shea's Gully, it was called – named after a guy named O'Shea who slipped and fell to his death. Not the best story to hear as you're struggling up the steep incline. After we eventually got up the other side of the gully, I had to pause a moment to catch my breath – as did the majority of the group. I looked back down and could see all the different areas of the path we had already climbed. Thank God, I thought, not long to go! I still managed to pose for a quick snap at the top of the gully. Looking back at it now, I don't look that tired, but I sure felt it!

It was a short climb up a slope – thankfully not as steep as O'Shea's Gully, but still a little painful on the legs! I had a sudden burst of energy and powered on up.

The wooden cross that was erected at the summit was a welcome sight by the time we got there and I felt extremely pleased to have gone through with the climb. Even more so, I was grateful for going in a group with friends. It was a good experience, and felt like a good old-fashioned pilgrimage where they would travel in small groups – safety in numbers. It wasn't an overly difficult walk – I have done worse – but it was nice to share the experience with others. I plonked my backpack down and grabbed a perch on one of the many boulders scattered around the summit (you had to be careful not to sit down on a sharp one). I gulped down a much-needed drink of water and paused to take in the beauty all around me. We weren't the only people at the summit – there were heaps of other groups and a few solo climbers also drinking in the spectacular scenery!

The highest peak in all of Ireland. I had climbed it and completed another part of the Irish pilgrim trail. On a good day, you get sweeping views over theMacgillycuddy's Reeks and the lakes below, including Caragh Lake. We were lucky the weather was good, and in between shrouds of cloud our view swept down the sides of the mountain and over the Irish countryside. I got a brief glimpse of a steel grey-blue in the distance in between the clouds that couldn't make their minds up whether they were staying or going– the Atlantic Ocean! I felt pretty chuffed seeing that. Now I had seen it from three out of the four points of the compass – north in Greenland, west in the United States and east in Ireland. I peered over the edge and I could see back down to the zig-zag track we had walked to reach the summit. There was a group from the Irish Cancer Society doing a fundraising walk up Carrauntoohil the same day as us who were a really neat group of people. We all took photos of each other under the cross marking the summit. We had one last glance around before we were rounded up to begin our descent back to Cronin's Yard. I hadn't even got to the bottom of Carrauntoohil and I was already planning the next part of the Irish pilgrim trails I wanted to see.

Carrauntoohill and my climbing companions Ina, Sophie and John

Carrauntoohill rocks and tarns

Carrauntoohill tarn, and myself almost at the summit

Carrauntoohill views and tarns

The summit at last!

The top of Carrauntoohill with Ina, John and the Irish Cancer Society

BURREN

One of the last places I made time to visit was the Burren, back up in County Clare. The Burren plateau is the largest area of karst topography (caves and sinkholes formed in easily dissolvable rock) in Europe. Vast stony plains with rock walls snaking in all directions; the scenery will leave you speechless. Rocks jut up from the ground and the area is home to alpine flowers and plants. Trees or any shrubbery are scarce here, and there are historic wedge tombs as on the Aran Islands.

There are quite a few pilgrim trails that run through the area and I walked some of these. The most popular is the Rath/Dysert Pilgrim Trail and every year there is a celebration held here in appreciation of ancient Irish pilgrims. The rocky landscape slopes down towards the coast and then drops sharply into the ocean. I thought it was quite an unusual landscape, but beautiful all the same.

Though it might be the largest area of karst in Europe, the whole area of the Burren is only fifteen square kilometres, which also makes it the smallest national park in Ireland. There are fresh water springs, woodlands, grasslands and petrified forests– it's a veritable feast for the eyes. While I was out walking, I found larger stone tombs. No one knows how they were constructed, as the roofs on some of the tombs weighed over a hundred tonnes each. There are over two hundred of these tombs around the Burren, including some in outdoor museums. They reminded of the houses in the old cartoon *The Flintstones*. One tomb that archaeologists have excavated revealed 22 people buried there; 16 adults and 6 children. So, we know why they were constructed, but not how!

The Burren is not only famous for these ancient tombs, but all the rare species of plants that are only found here. I found an interesting little perfumery located in the Burren. The Burren Perfumery began in 1972 and has a romantic story behind it. A lady named Sadie helped nurse Ralph, a visitor, to health after he fell from his horse. They fell in love and created the perfumery together. Everything is created on-site using local flowers. It was quite a special place.

The Burren

The Burren including an old wedge tomb

The Burren: Fanore Beach

The Burren with another tomb, limestone strata, and wild flowers

CHAPTER FOUR

Scotland – Picts, Druids, Celts and Christians

Scotland mostly escaped Roman rule. Inhabited in early days by Picts, thought to have been a local variety of Celt, and Britons (similar to Welsh), early Scotland was then settled by Norse from Norway, Gaels from Ireland bringing Gaelic (known in Latin as 'Scoti') and Northumbrians, whose Anglo-Saxon evolved into the Scots language or dialect of Robbie Burns (Lallans).

Scotland emerges as coherent state in 800s and 900s CE

Increasing English and French influence in Middle Ages. Edward I of England tries to annex Scotland, beaten off by William Wallace and Robert the Bruce, early 1300s.

Personal union of thrones with England, 1603. Act of Union to form Kingdom of Great Britain, 1707. Unsuccessful Jacobite (anti-Union) rebellions 1715, 1719, 1745.

Formerly poor, Scotland is transformed by Industrial Revolution, 1800s

Scottish timeline

SCOTLAND's history alone is reason enough to visit. The wild highlands and stories of red-headed Celts sending raiding parties to the Roman front lines – it's enough to get anyone even slightly interested to visit. My very first ever visit to Scotland was with my then fiancé, Niels, in 1984. I was amazed at how similar it was to New Zealand, and I could clearly see why the Scots liked coming to New Zealand. I saw remnants of Hadrian's Wall just over the border in England, which the Romans built to keep the wild inhabitants of the region they called Caledonia, now Scotland, out of the part of Britain that they ruled. In reality, the less wild ones were admitted through a form of passport control at the gates in the wall; then as now, such barriers were seldom absolute, and were more intended to regulate things.

That first time I was there I also learnt about the Picts, who are generally thought to have been a northerly group of Celts of the non-Gaelic sort, of whom the last sizeable remaining populations today consist of the Welsh and the Bretons. The Romans described the Picts as having tattooed or painted marks over their bodies, whence 'Pict' as in 'Picture': this is actually a Latin term and presumably not what the Picts called themselves. The Picts are thought to have merged with other groups, including the Gaels, by the 10th century CE, but they left many monuments behind in the form of carved

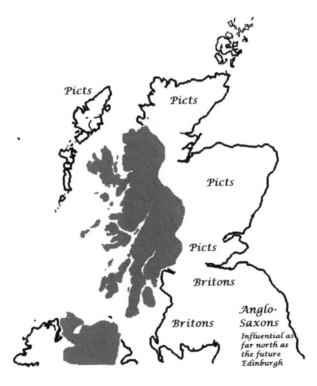

The settlement of Scotland around 500 CE, with the Gaelic (Irish) kingdom of Dalriada in grey. It was through Dalriada that the Gaelic language came.

stones. I was lucky enough to see Pictish stones on the West Highlands Walkway.

Scotland has plenty of historical value to me for its pilgrim trails, ruins and stories. I find all the myths and stereotypes surrounding the Scottish people interesting; were they, or weren't they, descended from Vikings? Were they as fierce and red-headed as people think? My journey through Scotland would show me first-hand some of the answers to these questions.

However wild they are, the Scots have given the world some amazing things like the flushing toilet, the sport of golf and the Glasgow Kiss – although I hope I never receive one!

Scotland Today

DUNDEE

As I mentioned before, I am of Scottish descent, and many of my father's family still live in Scotland. I hold both a British and a New Zealand passport, so coming and going through the British Isles is quite easy for me. Accommodation in Scotland has also never been a problem; I'd stay with aunties, uncles and cousins.

My paternal grandfather was John Walker, born and raised in Dundee. I find it interesting that he was never given a middle name. He married my grandmother, Mary (whom I am named after), who was from Edinburgh. My father used to tell me stories about his childhood growing up in Dundee. Once he went to a concert at Caird Hall in Dundee to see Frank Sinatra live. It was 13 July 1953, and he remembers that the concert wasn't a sell-out. In fact, there were fewer than 600 people who attended that concert. In his earlier years, my father, Brian, used to box and once fought a man named Dick McTaggart who went on to become quite famous. Dick McTaggart represented Scotland at the 1956 Melbourne Olympic Games where he won a gold medal in the lightweight boxing division, and at the 1960 Olympics in Rome where he won bronze.

My mother's father, a New Zealander with the surname of Kessell, used to drive around in an old 1930s Austin 10 right up until the day he died in 1980. When I was three years old I was playing in that car and fell out, leaving me with two scars above my eyes that I still have to this day.

I have been to Scotland many times since 1984 but it is always nice to come back, too, not just for my familial ties but also because of the culture there. I found that since I had been in Dundee last, the inner city had been developed so much and was all very impressive.

In fact, I am impressed with many things in Scotland. There are some well-preserved settlements from the Neolithic period in the Orkney Islands called Skara Brae, dating back from 3,180 BC to 2,500 BC. The oldest stone house in Europe is also found in Orkney, and is called the Knap of Howar. Orkney and the Shetland Islands were once actually part of Norway.

My first port of call on a recent trip was to go and stay with my Aunty June who lived in Dundee, Scotland. While I was in Dundee, my Aunty June was going through some of grandmother Mary's things and came across her birth certificate. There was an address for her home in Leith, an old harbour town about three kilometres north-east of downtown Edinburgh, nowadays a suburb, where she had lived as a child. We decided we would go and see where she had lived and I actually walked past my grandmother's house. I felt really privileged to see where she had been born and raised.

EDINBURGH

I find Edinburgh to be a beautiful city, filled with a rich history and colourful characters. It's quite a compact town and the Old Medieval District is a great place to visit, as is the New Town: so-called because it was built in the eighteenth century, which is new by Scottish standards. Edinburgh has plenty of good lookout points on some of the hills within the city where you get sweeping views across the main city and out into the Firth of Forth. It's a fascinating contrast of old and 'new'.

Aunty June and I went to Edinburgh Castle while I was visiting her. Edinburgh Castle is one of my favourite places. We visited the St Margaret's Chapel, part of Edinburgh Castle, built in the twelfth century and one of the oldest surviving buildings built in Edinburgh. Edinburgh Castle is a rich layer-cake of history that I think everyone with some kind of a connection to Europe should visit in person. It's not just relevant to the Scottish culture but also to the Irish, English, French, Spanish and even Scandinavian cultures, elements of which are all intertwined with the history of the castle. I have lost count of the amount of times I have visited Edinburgh Castle, but let me tell you it never ceases to amaze and thrill me.

My grandmother had told Aunty June stories about how she, when she was a child, used to go to Edinburgh Castle and swing on the gates. I stood at the same gates for a little while and imagined what it would have been like for my grandmother to swing on them. I am one of those people who find it an honour to be walking in the same places that all these people in the past have done, from my own grandmother Mary through to far more famous historical figures such as Mary, Queen of Scots.

Mary, Queen of Scots, was a remarkable woman and technically a ruler the second she was born. I remember being in what had been the Queen's bedroom in Edinburgh Castle and I overheard two French people asking, 'Why is it all in French?' The answer is that Mary was brought up in France and married to the French king. She spent her life in France until the age of 18 when her husband died and she returned to her homeland, Scotland. So, French was once a common language at the court of Scotland. Then, sadly, like many in the Tudor era, she was beheaded by her cousin, Queen Elizabeth. Mary was Catholic, and Elizabeth was Protestant. I think religion is more than important in the history of Scotland and Britain, and to stand in a place that holds such historical and religious value was beyond humbling.

While I was in Scotland, they were preparing for the vote about whether Scotland should become independent or remain a part of Britain. I was hoping that they would become independent after all the bloody wars fought over their inclusion in an English-dominated state in the past.

While I was there I also went to the Fringe Festival held annually in Edinburgh, which I loved. The Fringe Festival began in the 1940s as an add-on to an official, but rather stuffy, festival of the arts held in Edinburgh. Like the legendary *Salon des Réfusés* in which the Impressionist painters exhibited in nineteenth-century Paris — a salon for art refused official exhibition on the grounds of being too garish, blurry and unrealistic — the Fringe Festival showcased the acts that didn't make it into the official Edinburgh festival. And just like the *Salon des Réfusés*, it soon acquired the reputation of being the more interesting place to hang out!

BEN NEVIS

I had talked with June about wanting to do as much trekking as I could and to add to my lifelong journey walking parts of the Camino de Europa. Ben Nevis and the West Highland Ways form part of these trails (considered pilgrimages) through Scotland – and as it just so happened, I was in Scotland!

Guesses are made that Christianity made its way into areas of Scotland via the Romans when they occupied Britain around 43 to 410 CE. Living in such close proximity to Ireland meant that Irish missionaries were probably responsible for spreading Christianity throughout Caledonia. They travelled around Scotland from the fifth century onwards spreading the gospel to Picts and other Celts and creating some of the pilgrim trails around Scotland.

Leith:

Top Photo: looking down the Water of Leith from Commercial Street, past the Ship on the Shore toward the Old Victoria Swing Railway Bridge

Bottom Photo: Merchant Navy Memorial, in front of the Hotel Malmaison

Calton Hill: the site of six monuments, an observatory, and the headquarters of the present government of Scotland (St Andrews House)

Edinburgh Castle and its many ornate fire-places, with Auntie June

The Royal Scots Greys Monument, Princes Street Gardens, in front of Edinburgh Castle

Holyrood Abbey, at the eastern end of the Royal Mile

'Triumphal Entry' to the baroque Holyrood Palace, adjacent to Holyrood Abbey. The coat of arms is of Scotland.

The Quadrangle in Holyrood Palace and a closer view of the
forecourt fountain which stands outside the triumphal entrance

Edinburgh Fringe Festival

Holyrood Palace triumphal entrance with forecourt fountain

Much like its neighbouring countries, Scotland had an unsteady relationship with religion. Early Scotland was still a collection of tribes and clans, not a united country by any means. When the Scottish did become somewhat united, they distanced their church from others in Britain and Ireland. The rise of the Anglo-Saxon period saw the distinct differences in Christianity in Scotland, Ireland and England. The Scots and Irish developed their own forms of Celtic Christianity, while England followed more closely with the Roman version that was brought to the British Isles by St Augustine of Canterbury.

The St Columba's Monastery is the oldest church in Scotland. The monastery was completed around the sixth century, so we know that there was some form of established Christianity in Scotland by this time. There would of course be big changes to the various branches of Christianity practiced in Scotland in the centuries to come, to the point that Scotland would become a Presbyterian stronghold. Just as there are just so many ways and routes across Europe and Britain, there are many branches of Christianity, which is only fitting, I suppose. Anyway, there appear to be many ruins of monasteries around Scotland showing a different style than any others found in Europe. I'm pretty sure I know where I inherited that maverick gene.

So, after not really a whole lot of discussion, June and I had decided we would walk Ben Nevis together. It's spur-of-the-moment ideas and decisions that make life exciting, right?

We hired a car to visit Fort William, the home of ice-climbing in Scotland, in the depths of the highlands on the western coast of Scotland. The drive from Dundee to Fort William would take us through the lowlands of the Scottish countryside into the Northwest Highlands, an almost three-hour drive. Fort William is a popular holiday town for locals and tourists alike. Perched between the two waters of Loch Linnhe and Loch Eli, Fort William and its environs are breathtakingly beautiful. Fort William sits beneath the Ben Nevis Range at a bend in a long lake known as Loch Ell, which joins a seawater fiord called Loch Linnhe at a narrows only about 250 metres across, which in spite of its narrowness is not bridged but crossed by the Corran Ferry: an indication of how remote this area is. Fort William is only a few kilometres from the top of Ben Nevis as the crow flies. I found it quite interesting that Gaelic is still spoken here by some of the local population.

While we were there, we first headed down Loch Ell and Loch Linnhe by road to Oban, at the seaward end of Loch Linnhe, bound for the Isle of Iona where King Macbeth of Scotland is buried: the same Macbeth as is portrayed in William Shakespeare's play Macbeth. Iona lies within the Inner Hebrides group of islands, all of which are accessed by ferries and aircraft from Oban.

Iona features prominently in the history of Scottish monasticism and of this there is evidence in Latin and Gaelic, among other languages. The Iona Abbey was a monastery founded by an exiled Irish monk. This monastery was used to convert the Picts to the Christian faith and was a major area for Christian religion until the Vikings began raiding the Isle of Iona in 794 CE. Back then it was, and it still is today, a popular site for pilgrims to visit because of its great impact on spreading Christianity to the Scots and beyond. Quite a few prominent religious texts were written here by the monks on the island.

The actual burial place of King Macbeth was quite mesmerising. Macbeth was laid to rest in the cemetery which lies right behind the small stone St Oran chapel. The area is encompassed by a stone wall and looks out over the ocean. It was full of stone slabs indicating other people's final resting places.

I was amazed that such a small island had such religious significance that royalty such as Macbeth and supposedly another forty-seven kings from all over Europe were buried. After spending a few hours there, though, I could see why; for I found the Isle of Iona quite peaceful.

Climbing Ben Nevis had never been very high on my to-do list, but it all came with my interest in hiking and I was on a bit of a roll with mountains at the time. I later discovered that just like Carrauntoohil, climbing Ben Nevis is part of the pilgrim trails through Scotland. It's officially part of the West Highland Way walks. However, unlike Carrauntoohil, there isn't a lot of historical evidence to suggest that saints made their way here to spend time in prayer or fasting.

Ben Nevis is the highest mountain in all the British Isles. I really hadn't considered climbing it on this trip, but this is what I meant when I said you just seem to go with the flow and learn by events. Aunty June and I had got talking one night and then the next morning we were organising to climb Ben Nevis. Spontaneity probably accounts for the creation of some of my best memories.

So, my Aunty June borrowed some second-hand tramping boots (which really wasn't advisable) and then we booked into a hostel to stay. My cousin, her sons, were not too happy about her climbing Ben Nevis as they thought we would be doing a really difficult route, but we were taking the 'Mountain Track' which was the least difficult of the routes. One thing I remember about my Aunty June is that she has always loved taking videos of places she has been all over the world. She was turning 75 that year and going to climb Ben Nevis. I thought: 'Good on her. What a brilliant lady'.

Starting up Ben Nevis, with Auntie June's Taped-up Boots!

*The way up
Ben Nevis*

Ben Nevis, with a tarn

Ben Nevis summit including the observatory shelter

Ben Nevis with Summit Cairn and typical summit weather!

The height of Ben Nevis is only slightly higher than Carrauntoohil in Ireland, standing at 1,346 metres high. The mountain has some of the steepest faces in the UK, making parts of it really difficult to climb, for those who like difficult climbs. We had booked into a hostel for a night in Fort William, and there we met a German guy. He was just fantastic and he asked me if we wanted to climb with him as well. So, we did. I packed some tents to bring on the climb. We probably wouldn't need them, but Ben Nevis is known to have sudden dramatic changes in the weather that you would not want to get caught in. One minute it's cold, and then it's warm! Scotland has quite a cool climate and that is one factor I had to consider when I went trekking there.

Our trek would begin at the Glen Nevis carpark and rise quickly over rocky steps and narrow paths up the mountain's side. One hour into our trek and Aunty June's borrowed boots broke. She begged other walkers for tape and taped around her boots to hold them together. She was that determined to make it up the mountain. Sadly, Aunty June could not make it to the top with her taped-together boots, and so I my German climbing companion and I pressed on.

The walk was tough going – steep and rocky most of the way – but there were many beautiful waterfalls trickling down the sides. You definitely noticed the change in temperature as you got higher. And the closer we got to the summit, the harder it got to walk. Not because of the incline, but the ground was just a carpet of rock and stone. We did make it, though. Luckily, I had taken all my wet weather gear with me. When we reached the summit, it was freezing. We were greeted by torrential rain and I had to put on all my woollen and wet weather gear. I was so happy I had insisted on taking it with me. You climb all that way and the weather blocks all views!

Aunty June was quite disappointed with the trip, and I don't really blame her. We headed back down to Fort William and stayed in the hostel again to recover. The next day Aunty June headed back to Dundee by bus (and reassured my cousins she was fine!) I was going to stay on to do the West Highland Way. I stayed in Fort William in my tent that night, then drove to Kinlochleven, which was 30 minutes away.

The West Highland Way runs 154 kilometres through the Scottish Highlands. It is quite a popular walk and roughly 80,000 people walk parts of it every year. The route is quite hilly in places and follows ancient

The West Highland Way

trading routes, forming part of the Camino de Europa. In fact, in 2010 it became part of the International Appalachian Trail, another series of walks throughout the globe. The Highland Way is separated into different stages; the East and the West Highland Ways and then the Speyside Way in the north. The part I was going to do begins in Fort William at the base of Ben Nevis and goes right the way to Glasgow. I didn't have enough time to walk all the way to Glasgow, and I had my rental car, so I decided to walk from Kinlochleven to Fort William and a bit further. I had worked out I had about five days to spare.

I parked in a carpark in the centre of Kinlochleven and caught a train to the beginning of the walk. Kinlochleven was another pretty Scottish town perched on the banks of River Leven– hence its name, I guess. Kinlochleven, funnily enough, was the first village in the world to have every house connected to electricity. The 'electric village' they termed it. I would walk from here to the end of the trail and then catch a train or bus back to my car. It was about six hours to walk from Kinlochleven to Fort William. I found it was not very busy along that route, but I didn't mind that. When I first started, I met two guys who were from Kinlochleven. They were wearing traditional Scottish kilts – Black Watch Regiment kilts, they told me. They were having a bet with some other walkers and they lost it, and it was that they would complete the entire round trip back to Kinlochleven in their kilts.

*The West
Highland Way*

Setting up camp for the night near an abandoned house between Fort William and Kinlochleven

*The West Highland
Way continued*

The West Highland Way heading onwards

A cairn on the West Highland Way, next to the sign below, commemmorating the Battle of Inverlochy (1645). Tradition holds that MacDonalds should add a stone, Campbells take one away.

Wild Rocky Terrain on the West Highland Way

Kinlochleven

Bank St, Fort William

Cameron Square,
Fort William

The Laggan Dam and Loch Laggan, above Fort William and Kinlochleven

I had read quite a bit of information on the West Highland Way. Scotland has a 'Highland Tiger', *felis silvestris grampia*, the Scottish Wildcat, which I was hoping to see. From a distance, the Scottish Wildcat looks like a domestic cat of a stripy breed such as a tabby. But the Scottish Wildcat is quite a bit bigger than a domestic cat and it dines on creatures that a house-cat would normally be afraid to take on, such as full-grown rabbits.

Dogs that make the mistake of confusing a wildcat with a house-cat can also expect to be savaged. These differences mean that the wildcat is a cultural symbol of fearlessness to the Scots, as opposed to the house-cat which is notoriously timid. I don't think I ever saw one of these magnificent wildcats, however, as the one thing they do fear is humans. Elusive as they are round people, Scottish Wildcats will happily interbreed with domestic cats and that is actually the chief threat the wildcat faces. If feral house-cats become too numerous, the wildcats will be bred out and the rabbits, no doubt, will multiply.

The Western Highlands is also an area where there numerous Pictish sites – there were rocks everywhere that were historical evidence of the ancient people.

Roman accounts are often the only written ones we have of ancient peoples, such as the Picts, who lived on the frontiers of the Roman Empire, in territories such as Caledonia (Scotland) and Germania, which needs no translation. From Roman accounts, such people were wild, unruly and violent. Roman accounts are, of course, only 'one side of the story': a story often aimed at demonstrating the superiority of Roman civilisation.

Thus, the Romans tell us that from Caledonia to Germania the barbarians enjoyed knocking back ox-horns filled with beer while telling progressively taller and more ridiculous tales until fights broke out. These were habits that distinguished barbarians from civilised people who, of course, preferred to drink wine while discussing more rational topics.[1] The idea that beer is a suitable drink for 'barbarians' prone to boasting, exaggeration and brawls

---

[1] See for instance Nelson, Max. (2005). The Barbarian's Beverage: A History of Beer in Ancient Europe. http://scholar.uwindsor.ca/llcpub/26

while wine is more 'civilised' is a prejudice that's still very much alive and well today, untold centuries after the Empire fell in Western Europe.

Even ethnic prejudices in the Roman world were often directed against pale northerners. The classical Greeks and Romans regarded their appearance and many of their supposed qualities as conforming to a sort of golden mean *inter negrum et pallidum*. The northerners were held to be too pale (*pallidum*), the Africans too dark (*negrum*). The barbarians on both frontiers of the empire, northern and southern, supposedly ran to temperamental extremes caused in the final analysis by too little or too much exposure to sunshine. But the inhabitants of the Mediterranean world were supposed to be just right, well-balanced both in appearance and temperament, because they inhabited latitudes that were themselves just right for civilisation to flourish.

So, we have it on the authority of the Romans that the Picts were a bunch of barbarians. Well, to slightly misquote Mandy Rice-Davies, they *would* say that, wouldn't they?

I wonder what the Pictish language would have sounded like? It's thought that it was probably similar to modern-day Welsh. But nobody knows for sure. Perhaps we will never know.

In spite of the mysteriousness of the Picts, they left a surprising number of carved monuments and inscriptions behind. It was great to see some of these along the West Highland Way.

At Glencoe, near Kinlochleven, I saw a monument about the McGregor-Campbell feud. This was a legendary feud between two families in the 1600s, both laying claim to areas of land around Lorn and Breadalbane, just north of Glasgow. The Campbells had better or more successful political connections at the time and the McGregors very much got the worst of it. The McGregor surname was proscribed by law as far back as 1603 meaning that anyone who kept it could be killed. The proscription was lifted by Charles II, but was reimposed by William of Orange and his co-ruler Queen Mary, the McGregors having lately backed King James II of England, who was also James VII of Scotland, in the so-called Glorious Revolution of 1688, a revolution in which James was overthrown by William and Mary.

On the 13th of February 1692 thirty-eight surrendered McGregors, imagining themselves safe at last and enjoying the hospitality of their late enemies, were massacred in and around Glencoe in a notorious act of treachery, with about forty more dying of exposure after their houses were burned down. This was very embarrassing for William and Mary and the blame was pinned on local underlings including the leadership of the Campbells, though no-one was ever punished by law. Some McGregors survived as semi-outlaws, like the famous Rob Roy McGregor. The McGregors would continue to be persecuted by law until 1774.

The first night, I decided to make camp by some ruins that sat close by a stream. I pitched my tent and, my God, the midges! I went down to the stream to get some water for a cup of tea and I opened my mouth and thousands of midges (biting insects) went into my mouth. I guessed that was why the trail wasn't very busy just then! The midges there are ravenous. I put the window down in my car when I was with Aunty June on our way to Fort William and they all flew in the window. She told me to put the window up because they were swarming around her head and biting her.

The walk was quite relaxing, although challenging in some areas. It was about the third day on my walk when the rain started in the afternoon, and it was torrential. I stayed in my tent because of the weather for one night and a day. Although it could have turned into four or five days quite easily, I knew I had to continue on because I was running out of time. I was surprised that there were quite a few French people around. I was also surprised to find a lot of walkers camping in their tents along the way. Usually people book well in advance and stay in one of the many hostels in the towns you pass through.

There were plenty of sights of historical value through the walk. I stayed one night by an old stone house. I can't remember how old it was but it was really cool to see, and I set my tent up a few metres from it. Then there was the ancient Dun Deardail fort hidden away behind trees, which they were still excavating when I walked past. It is said to be remnants of a settlement from around the first millennium BCE to the first millennium CE, so it was ridiculously old! The hill overlooks Glen Nevis but it is still a mystery as to who built it.

By the end of it, I was glad I had done the walk – another spur-of-the-moment idea. I had climbed Ben Nevis and still had had the energy to do the West Highland Way, so I was quite glad I had been organised and taken all my walking gear with me to Ben Nevis. The West Highland Way was a great way to see the Scottish high country and walk through the many small towns in the area. I walked back to Kinlochleven and drove back to Aunty June's in Dundee.

FORT WILLIAM

On another trip to Fort William, I went with my cousins, Aunty June's sons. We had hired a boat to travel around on one of the lochs.

Loch, a Gaelic word for lake which can also mean fiord or marine inlet, is spelt Lough in Ireland; where it has the same broad meaning. There are some lochs and loughs in the north of England too. But fundamentally this is an Irish/Scottish term.

My cousins were avid soccer fans and supported the Rangers Football Club. There is quite a bit of history between the Rangers and Celtic soccer teams, as their foundations are built on the religious divide between Protestants and Catholics. Usually the Ranger's fans are Protestants and the Celtics are Catholics, but my cousins were brought up Catholic and supported the Protestant team instead.

The two teams have one of the longest standing rivalries (now over 100 years) yet they both claim Glasgow as their home ground. Religion just seems to have a part in everything – even football! Anyway, one day while we were on the loch, we decided to park up the boat and head into town to have a drink and something to eat at a local pub. My cousins were wearing their usual red and blue colours supporting Rangers (like I said, they were avid fans!) The one pub we went into was full of fans of the opposing team, Celtic. Well, let's just say, we didn't hang around long in that pub and I learnt just how deep that football rivalry ran. Both of my cousins almost got into a fight and were completely outnumbered. I grabbed them and headed for the door.

Travelling on the lochs was beautiful; one of the best ways to see Scotland. The lochs are interconnected through various waterways and so you can start on one and end up somewhere completely different. We met Aunty June and Uncle Dave in Fort William to go to a *ceilidh*, pronounced 'caley', a traditional Scottish-style dance party. It was my grandmother who taught me all about dancing; she'd get me out my Scottish Black Watch kilt and teach us how to do the Scottish Highland fling. I had a Black Watch regiment kilt because my grandmother's family had served in it at Edinburgh Castle. Rather ironically in view of the regiment's name, the kilt's colours were a pretty blue and green, quite bright, and I loved getting dressed up in one. Black Watch tartans can also be a lot darker. The darker versions served for concealment in the old days, a forerunner of camouflage. This is one theory as to the origin of the name Black Watch. We stayed for three days in Fort William and visited the Highland caves. There are quite a number of caves up in the hills in and around Fort William, and I imagined Picts hiding out in these caves during wars with the Romans.

While I was in Fort William I also tried my first haggis. All I can say is that it was a great experience... and I'll leave it at that!

One last thing: in Spain, I came across a book called the *Cantigas de Santa Maria*, which is written in both Portuguese and Galician and shows images of the bagpipe, one of Scotland's most iconic symbols. That surprised me: I thought we Scottish had a solid claim to inventing them. In fact, in turns out that pretty much everybody in Europe, North Africa, the Middle East and India has some sort of local tradition of the bagpipes even if they don't play them very much anymore; for in most countries the bagpipes ceased to be played as more modern musical instruments such as violins, brass instruments and oboes came along. Scotland is unusual for hanging onto the bagpipes: but Scotland didn't invent them.

The Germans call the bagpipes *Dudelsack*, that is to say tootle-sack or doodle-sack, which is as good a name as any. There is an amusing print from around 1530 by the German engraver Erhard Schön which shows the Devil playing a *Dudelsack* that looks like a monk's head, the meaning of it being something like the saying that 'the Devil quotes scripture'. And it is to Germany, and is neighbours Austria and Switzerland, that I now turn.

CHAPTER FIVE
Germany, Switzerland and Austria

Germany, Switzerland and Austria

GERMANY has an interesting history of pilgrimages. The Great German Pilgrimage probably being one of the most well-known. In the years 1064 and 1065, many people, led by Archbishop Siegfried of Mainz, Bishop William of Utrecht, Bishop Otto of Ratisbon and Bishop Gunther of Bamberg, went on a pilgrimage to Jerusalem. It wasn't an easy one, and they ran into plenty of trouble and bandits along the way. In fact, many

Like Scotland, most of Germany was never incorporated into the Roman Empire and remained a land of 'barbarians' (just like Scotland).

Germany split from France (land of the Franks, Germanic invaders of the Roman Empire) by Treaty of Verdun in 843 CE. Germany often referred to, misleadingly, as Holy Roman Empire (HRE) until 1806.

Swiss Confederation established by mountain-dwellers seeking independence from the HRE

Fall of HRE ('First Empire') leads eventually to Second German Empire 1870-1918 and also to Austrian Empire 1804-1918.* Austria and Germany not totally distinct hitherto.

Third Empire ('Reich' in German) unusually disastrous. Eventually Germany, Switzerland and Austria all become model democracies.

* Austro-Hungarian Empire from 1867

German pilgrims were attacked en-route to the Holy Land and it was the beginning of the end of pilgrimages from Europe to Jerusalem and their replacement by crusades.

Christianity in Germany traces back to Roman rule and flourished after the fourth century. The part of Germany west of the Rhine and south of the Danube was controlled by the Roman Empire during its peak, and after the decay of the Roman Empire, then so too did the Christian faith crumble. After Clovis, the King of the Franks, a German tribe that gave its name to France, was baptised a Catholic in 508 CE the Christian religion was reintroduced to the area. Following this, Irish, English and Scottish Missionaries reintroduced Catholicism to German people. There were also still pagan influences, notably Norse mythology, which was widespread during the Viking era.

The most important pilgrim walk for me was the *Jakobsweg*, which is the German term for '[St] James's Way'. It begins in Nürnberg (Nuremberg) and ends in the town of Konstanz, which we generally term Constance, a lakeside town at the southern extremity of Germany. The *Jakobsweg* is broken into sections because it is so long. There is the Palatine section, which passes by Speyer and a Benedictine Abbey. Another is known as the Northern Route, not to be confused with the one of the same name in Spain. This alternative path goes through Neustadt an der Weinstrasse and Landstuhl, finishing up at Hornbach Abbey. Then there is the Monks' Trail, which follows a historical pathway from Glücksstadt on the River Elbe to the island of Fehmarn in the Baltic Sea. This path is dedicated to retracing the steps of some of the very first Christian missionaries into Germany. Many people cycle this because it is a 342-kilometre journey.

There are two important pilgrim sites found along the Spree River in Germany: the Franciscan Abbey of Bornhofen and the St Apollinaris Church. The Abbey is run by monks and has the Statue of Our Lady of Sorrows of Bornhofen which dates back to the fourteenth century. The Abbey is located in Kamp-Bornhofen and open to tourists to view. The St Apollinaris Church is a grand piece of neo-gothic architecture and sits overlooking the Rhine River. It is home to a famous Christian relic of St Apollinaris.

All the pathways go past fascinating churches with relics hundreds of years old and past gravesites of saints who lived well before our time. From where the trails reach the borders of Germany into countries like Austria and France, it still leaves the pilgrim with around 2,600 kilometres to walk to Santiago de Compostela in Spain. An incredible journey, particularly for the medieval pilgrims.

There are just so many pilgrimages that can be made throughout so many different countries around Europe. I can see why the Camino de Europa is known as the grandmother of all caminos – there are probably hundreds that connect up and all lead to the St James's way in Spain. In this way, Germany became an important part of my pilgrim journey.

FRANKFURT

My very first visit to Germany was part of a Eurobus trip that I did around Europe in the 1990s. My first stop was Frankfurt and I remember all the beautiful window displays in the bakeries, fishmongers and butchers. The shopkeepers really put a lot of effort in.

Frankfurt is a bustling metropolis with high-rises and skyscrapers in the city centre. I wasn't really expecting it to be so modern and upbeat – it was a fun place to be for a traveller! Frankfurt has lots of squares and paved areas for pedestrians only – great for shopping and looking around without worrying about cars and motorbikes zooming past. There are areas of the city that are more historical than others and have some grand examples of German history. In some parts, you will have a cute little medieval townhouse opposite a busy café and clothing store. I quite liked the contrast which made it all the more interesting! By night it is a glittering skyline of lights, and there are loads of museums and art galleries littered throughout the city. The restaurants and bars were great too. Trains and trams seemed to be the main modes of transportation around Frankfurt and are quite impressive! The main city centre lies on either side of the Rhine River and it is easy enough to walk around and find your way. The vibe in Frankfurt was cool, fun and quite youthful at the time! I enjoyed being there with my Eurobus travelling companion, Belinda.

I spent time in the city centre using buses and the subway, but most of my exploration was done on foot, of course! I didn't have much time up my sleeve, but my usual motto is to do and see as much as I can – so I did! I wound up at the Old St Nikolai church – this fascinating building was so typical of the Gothic German style built in the mid-fifteenth century, on the site of an old chapel originally erected in the twelfth century. You can take guided tours through it, but I didn't have the time or a whole lot of money to throw at things like that (I was on the backpacking budget then), so I just wandered around the outside and admired the exterior! Another place I remember visiting quite vividly was the Archaeological Garden right in the heart of Frankfurt. It was a solid reminder of how much I loved learning about the history of places. It is a collection of historic remains, including an old Roman palace and baths (with heating) which were built somewhere in the first and second centuries, and a Roman wall and medieval houses among a few other old structures as well.

Visiting the historical sites in Frankfurt became part of my pilgrimage through Germany and probably incorporated a few different routes into my own one. The pilgrim trails in Germany stack up to hundreds and thousands of kilometres, crossing over the borders into neighbouring countries and continuing on to Italy and Spain. Eventually they all connect up.

I caught a bus through one part of the series of pilgrim trails, as I didn't have the energy to walk the 95.4km to Heidelberg, another part of the German St James's way. My ticket for the Eurobus was only valid for a year and I reckon I could have spent the entire year just walking the pilgrim routes in Germany, so I did have to speed up a few parts of my journey – there was still so much to see!

HEIDELBERG

Heidelberg was a gorgeous country town – romantic, quaint, picturesque and just plain old cute! The bus trip from Frankfurt was fast (a little over an hour), and it was nice to sit back and relax after the hustle and bustle in Frankfurt. I had a window seat on the bus, so I had good views over the countryside between the two towns. I was really amazed by all the stunning period buildings. It was all very medieval and rustic and I could see why this section of the trail was referred to as the romantic route.

The Heidelberg Castle, which looks over the Neckar River, is an important stop for pilgrims and home to the famous Heidelberg Tun (a large wine barrel). The castle holds important religious significance to the Protestant branches of Christianity, and I found out that Heidelberg is a particularly popular spot for Protestant pilgrimages. The German branch of Protestantism is known as Lutheranism and was founded by Martin Luther in the 1500s. This German branch, also prominent in Scandinavia, is said to have over 74 million members following the faith today.

I remember walking around and being surprised at the university there. It is one of the oldest in Germany and is an exquisite building. It seemed to be quite the popular tourist attraction in the town; people were taking photos and wandering around the grounds.

I had time to check out the 'Old Town', a part of town that was a tribute to the Baroque period of architecture. There are loads of little marketplaces, narrow lanes and squares, which were always populated with foot traffic. They had some cute little cafes that I stopped in to get my coffee fix. As for the castle, it is one of the most famous ruins in Europe. The town was sacked in 1622 during the Thirty Years War and again in 1689 during the Nine Years War, also known as the Palatine War. Four years later the castle suffered further damage by the French, and in 1764 what was left of it was struck by lightning and burned down. The town was rebuilt but the castle was not. Today. Heidelberg is a beautiful place with all the romantic vibes you'd expect of a small, German country town.

I had heard people talking about the wild Siberian geese that frequented the area in the warmer months – I didn't get to see any but that would have been interesting! I decided I would take a quick trip over the Austrian border to a small town called Innsbruck.

INNSBRUCK, AUSTRIA

I caught a train to Innsbruck, a city in western Austria. It sits just below the Nordkette or 'north chain' mountain ranges. This was another area populated by the Romans and remnants of this survive through the use of Roman names for towns and cities in Austria. The importance of the Romans being here, there and everywhere shows how far Catholicism and Christianity were spread. They created, and were the basis of, many of the pilgrim trails that began around Europe.

Innsbruck is a popular ski town, and I loved it – I thought it was a beautiful place, surrounded by snow-capped peaks and ranges. I took a cable car up to one of the ski fields and did a bit of skiing in the Nordkette ranges. I made friends with a group of students visiting from China who were really interesting! Apparently, Innsbruck is quite a popular area for international students to stay and study. While I was up on the mountain, I saw some men in plus-fours knee-britches! I hadn't seen anyone wear them before – they reminded me of my grandfather, who had some. I also saw a lot of black ravens hanging around on the top. They were huge and had sleek, glossy feathers, which were almost blue-black. It was also while I was there that I saw farmers working the land by hand and using pitchforks to make hay – it was amazing and I admired them for being so hard-working!

The St James Trail of Tirol winds through Austria to connect up with the other ways in other countries that eventually lead to Santiago de Compostela. It is incredible to think people would venture out to travel such a long distance for the sake of penance or other religious reasons. It would have been incredibly taxing on the body, and dangerous as well in those days.

To the east of Innsbruck is small town called Absam, another stop along the St James pilgrims trail. I made a brief visit to the village and parish church as part of my Camino de Europa trip. This town became a site of pilgrimage because in 1797, as happened in many other popular places along the pilgrim trails at different times, there was an apparition of Mary and it was the site of many miracles.

I found it to be a quaint little town and there was an air of spirituality within the village. There were other pilgrims here as well; some on foot and some on bikes. My trip was only brief and I had to head back to Germany soon. It was great to see part of the area that belongs to the St James Trail through Austria.

BERLIN

It was in the 1990s when I first laid eyes on Berlin, and I was truly blown away. They were still tearing down the Berlin Wall and that gave it a bit of a dull vibe; everything was grey, dusty, dirty and being demolished. Berlin had just gone through a difficult process reuniting the East and the West sections of Berlin. The difficulty was that because of the division created by the Berlin Wall between the East and West, it had established differences in the urban cultures and two very distinct cultural groups emerged. While this is being remedied, there is still some evidence of two different groups today.

I visited a second time some years later and I could see the amazing progress and changes that had occurred since my last visit. I felt that this time around Berlin was vibrant, and I enjoyed being there more this time. I also noticed a big change in the people. Young people were moving into Berlin encouraged by the rent freeze that the government had imposed on

Berlin landlords. Germany needed to heal and they didn't want Berlin to be another city that its own people couldn't afford to live in. I thought it was a great idea and I'm not sure very many other countries would do that for their people.

I loved Berlin at night – gone were the oppressive pubs and their vibes, now replaced by more sophisticated restaurants; but at the same time you now had to pay to use a toilet which had not been the case before. When I did go into one I wasn't too happy that the toilet seat was dirty, as they had charged €1 to use it. You could go to bars with swimming pools and sand all around them. There were bands playing in the streets, and I noticed Berlin was becoming quite a popular art and music scene. You could go down to the Spree River and there were many good public spaces to make use of and hang out. I found that Germans loved their public spaces. I would see them all lying along the river banks at night time and just spending time in the places allocated to public use.

By night Berlin was a stunning city filled with people from all over the world. It was exciting! I found people in Berlin to be tolerant, kind and friendly. They were open to other cultures and I detected no racism while I was staying there. I didn't get any special attention for being a New Zealander, either – they just seemed to treat everyone the same!

One thing I noticed particularly in Berlin was the acceptance of nudity. Being nude in public was ok! In fact, there are quite a number of public areas around the city where you can just go and be naked; it's not a big deal there. Berlin also has an international School of Nudism to encourage bare skin exercising. It was especially popular in the former East Germany, where it had hippie-like connotations of rebellion against the system and where there were many areas allocated to nudism or as it is known in German *Freikörperkultur* or FKK, 'free body culture'. Attitudes in the former West

Germany were much more prudish. There was a bit of it when I had visited re-united Germany previously, but since then it must have really taken off! There are clubs dedicated to *Nacktjoggen*, or naked jogging. While you won't find me in any of these areas, it is all quite interesting. United by nakedness in Berlin.

I did a lot of sightseeing around Berlin in 2008 and 2015. I saw the Bundeswaschmaschine, the Brandenburg Gate and the Berlin Hauptbahnhof. A new chancellery building next to the Reichstag is called the Bundeswaschmaschine, 'Federal Washing Machine' because of its round windows. The old-fashioned, neoclassical Reichstag building meanwhile sports a modern, transparent dome on top which looks slightly incongruous as well.

The Brandenburg Gate was an impressive sight. It is an 18th-century monument, and one of the most well-known in Germany. It is now associated with the tearing down of the Berlin Wall and the reunification of Germany: effectively it is now the symbol of modern Germany. I remember looking up at the huge columns and the massive statues on the top; it was a beautiful piece of history and one that would be so much more important to the people now.

The Berlin Hauptbahnhof is the main railway station in the city. It too had been extensively renovated since I had last visited.

DRESDEN

In 2015, I had been invited to stay in Dresden by a German woman named Anna whom I had met in New Zealand. Anna had come to Queenstown a few years ago and was staying at my friend's house via the Couchsurfing website. We had a good time showing Anna around and getting out and about in Queenstown. Before Anna had left, she offered for me to stay at

*The Brandenburg Gate is an entrance into the urban core of Berlin via
a huge park called the Tiergarten. On the other side, traffic used to enter
an urban square surrounded by buildings, called Pariser Platz.*

All images Wikimedia Commons. Photographic collage consists of details from
Max Siegmayer, 'Straße des 17. Juni von der Siegessäule aus fotografiert', 10
September 2015, CC-BY-SA 4.0. Lower image is a painting made in 1915 by
Ernst Ludwig Kirchner, 'Brandenburger Tor', reproduction in public domain.

By an odd coincidence of history, the gate which had long marked an internal boundary between town green belt and urban core found itself on another boundary in the Cold War, between East and West Berlin. Pariser Platz became a wide-open no-man's-land, its war-damaged buildings demolished and not rebuilt.

Images Wikimedia Commons. Top photograph, taken in the late 1970s, released into public domain by Elżbieta Glanc-Boteva; bottom photograph, taken in 1983, released into the public domain by 'Jeffchat1'.

Pariser Platz today. The buildings are back. In the background can be seen the Reichstag and in the far background the new Chancellery, the 'Bundeswaschmaschine'.

Images Wikimedia Commons. Top photograph Berthold Werner, 30 March 2011, CC-BY- SA 3.0; Bottom photograph by 'Heinzi', 11 September 2010, CC-BY-SA 3.0.

These days the immediate environs of the gate are pedestrianised on both side, making the area a natural party and concert venue with the Tiergarten as backdrop. In the upper photograph, an illuminated stage faces the Tiergarten as seen from a rebuilt Pariser Platz. In the lower photograph, a chain of lights commemorates where the Berlin Wall used to go.

Brandenburg Gate during the 'Festival of Lights'.
Detail from photograph by Michael F. Mehnert, Wikimedia
Commons, 23 October 2009, CC-BY-SA 3.0.

her place in Dresden when I next came to Germany. So, before I had left
New Zealand I had got in touch with her and organised to stay with her
in Dresden.

Dresden is the capital of the Free State of Saxony, a federal state in
Germany near the border with the Czech Republic. The River Elbe runs
right through the centre of it and is quite a key feature of Dresden with a lot
of dedicated places to go along the river banks. Bombing during World War
II had completely destroyed the inner city, killing thousands of people, so
I found Dresden to be in a state of construction as well. I also learnt about
how the English language actually originated as a West Germanic language,

which was interesting: whence official English light vs. Scottish / German *licht*, and milk in modern English versus *milch* in older forms of English and as it happens, in modern German too. Of course, there are many French and Latin words in English as well, and indeed loan-words of all sorts.

I found Anna's house, and we got on our bikes and did a lot of biking around the city. Everyone seemed to make use of their bikes and that's how everyone got around in Dresden (which I had noticed as well in Berlin). Dresden was pretty cool – there was a lot going on there and the buildings were great. They had some good outdoor public spaces around too, which people made good use of. They were always busy, with Germans just hanging out – and I'm sure there were a few nudist areas here as well. There were a lot of anti-immigration protests and marches happening at the time – so different from what I had experienced in Berlin City. People were getting a bit frustrated with the government's changes. Anna mentioned to me that if eastern Germany had still been under Communist rule, she could have retired comfortably at 55 from her occupation as a teacher. The retirement age had been raised to 67 and wages hadn't increased either. Also, housing had not been an issue for teachers as it was supplied under the Communists, whereas now it was a problem.

I had an understanding of teaching from when I had worked as a teacher in New Zealand. Anna said some people wondered what it would have been like to still have communist rule in eastern Germany. One thing I did admire about Germany, and I noticed it most in Dresden, was the ability to completely rebuild a city. The old buildings had been restored, and I later saw similar restoration ongoing in the former Soviet Union.

We did actually spend a lot of our time sightseeing on a bike. I remember going out one day on my own and I started to get a bit hungry. I saw a massive building all done out in red and saw the word 'Turkish' on the outside. I thought, 'Great, a Turkish kebab shop'. In New Zealand, there are many Turkish restaurants and kebab shops – we are pretty spoilt for choice. So, I parked my bike outside and went in. It was quite dimly lit in the shop and I could see people smoking tobacco down the back of the room. I did a quick scan around the room and saw it was mostly men. My stomach was in charge then, and I didn't think anything of it so went up to the counter. I asked for a kebab, much to the disdain of the shop owner. He frowned at me and it was then I realised I had walked into a Turkish men's club. Oops! By the look on all their faces that hadn't happened before. I left and told Anna about it. We laughed about it for ages.

People seem to love their folk music in Germany. They get right into it and have a lot of festivals and street music to celebrate. I enjoyed the whole atmosphere of Dresden; it seemed things were really going ahead there. I saw in some old German porcelain in a museum. Centuries ago, the Germans found a way to make similar, if not better, quality porcelain than the Chinese. A factory was commissioned by Augustus II the Strong, Elector of Saxony, in Meissen, just outside of Dresden, in 1720. This factory was commissioned to create massive porcelain sculptures for the Japanese Imperial palace in the form of various animals. It was quite remarkable, considering porcelain was first invented by the Chinese.

I found everyone liked to lie on the banks of the River Elbe at night in groups or on their own. People just seemed to enjoy being outdoors and really made the most of inner city pedestrian terraces and esplanades on both sides of the Elbe. Anna told me there had been quite a big uproar caused by a wealthy West German who had wanted to develop part of this area for apartments just after the reunification. People had got quite upset and it led to protests that saved the public space in its entirety.

SAXON SWITZERLAND

I had had enough of being in a city and was ready for some fresh air, so I went by train from Dresden to Saxon Switzerland National Park. I had heard it has some of the most beautiful trekking in the world. The landscapes went from rocky to thick forest and the views at the summits were amazing. The region extends across the border into the Czech Republic, where it is known as the Bohemian (i.e., western Czech) Switzerland.

The Elbe Sandstone Mountains run throughout this national park, with the highest peak at 723 metres above sea level. The trail I was going to do meant getting to the Dresden train station (Bahnhof Dresden Neustadt), and catching a train to Schöna.

This brought me to the beginning of the trail at Stadt Wehlen that went to Rauensteine. After that walk, I took a ferry called the Rathen Bastei, which has been on the River Elbe since 1911. It is a successor to earlier boats dating back to the 17th century, that used the currents to move to their destination.

I also got see the beautiful Bastei Bridge as part of the trail. The Bastei Bridge is a stone pedestrian bridge through rocky pillars. When you walk to the top you get beautiful views over the park. After the Bastei Bridge I got back on the ferry and followed another trail to Rathen. I took the train from here back to Dresden. Saxon Switzerland was only thirty kilometres from Dresden, so the trip was brief.

With so many mentions of Saxons, I did get a bit confused as I had been brought up to think of Saxons as people who lived in England a long time ago, not people who lived in the present day and age in the heart of Europe. But by the end of my travels I had most of it figured out.

Two classic eighteenth-century paintings of Dresden by Bernardo Bellotto, also known as Canaletto. The top painting shows a panorama of Dresden as seen from the right bank of the Elbe below the Augustus Bridge (1748), the second (1765) the collapsed ruins of the old Kreuzkirche (Church of the [Holy] Cross), which fell down as a result of damage suffered in the Seven Years' War: war damage is nothing new for cities such as Dresden.

Both paintings downloaded as public domain images from the Google Art Project. The panorama is held in the Gemäldegalerie Alte Meister, Dresden; the Kreuzkirche painting is held at the Kunsthaus Zürich (a similar one is also held in the Gemäldegalerie Alte Meister).

Dresden panoramas showing the famous, elevated, Brühl Terrace.

All Wikimedia Commons. Top image by Rene Schwietzke, 1 Sept. 2004, CC-BY-2.0. Middle image by 'DrTorstenHenning', 21 Sept. 2005, public domain. Bottom image public domain, circa 1900, accession LC-DIG-ppmsca-00953, Library of Congress.

Dresden Frauenkirche (Church of our Lady) and view from the Frauenkirche over the Elbe showing the statue of Fama on the Cupola of the Kunstakademie (Art School) Dresden with the Carola and Albert bridges in background, below.

Dresden by Night

The original Saxons, whose name meant 'people of the *Seax*', a lengthy war-knife which many of them carried, were a Germanic tribe who along with the closely related Jutes and Angles inhabited the North Sea coasts of modern Germany, the Netherlands and the Jutland peninsula of Denmark in Roman times. After the departure of the Roman legions from Britain in 410 CE, the Angles, Jutes and Saxons moved into Great Britain and became known as the Anglo-Saxons. At the same time, strong cultural and trading links were maintained with stay-at-home Jutes, Angles and Saxons. Over time Jutland became taken over by the Danes, a somewhat different people; and the Saxons who had not moved to Britain also spread into the interior of Germany.

It was a really interesting and knowledge-filled journey through Germany, and I felt like I was connecting all the dots and making good progress with the Camino de Europa.

SWITZERLAND

And then of course there is the real Switzerland, which I crossed into by train from France after climbing Mont Blanc (as described in Chapter 7), before heading on to Italy: an eventful train trip that I also describe in *A Maverick Traveller*. I wanted to see Geneva before I doubled back south to attempt Monte Viso (Chapter 10). Even though Mont Blanc and some of the other parts of the French alps I visited at the time weren't very far from Monte Viso, I also needed a break from alpinism.

In Switzerland, I marvelled at how clean everything was. It was all quite prim and proper. While I was there, though, I managed to sit in on a parliamentary meeting in one of the churches, St Paul's. I thought this a bit odd because Switzerland is a secular state – meaning Switzerland has no state religion – so why would they hold it in a church? It was in any case quite a busy affair and a few of the public where sitting in on it too.

I did like Geneva. I saw the Jet d'Eau fountain and did a ferry ride around Lac Léman (Lake Geneva). Half the lake is in Switzerland and the other half is in France! I wonder if you need a passport to cross into the French side of the water.

Geneva is, of course, home to the United Nations Headquarters. I wandered around the square that had a neat sculpture called the Broken Chair. Geneva had some great outdoor spaces with lots of fountains and sculptures around.

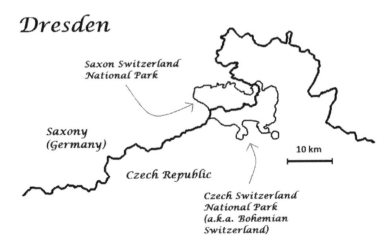

The Saxon and Bohemian Switzerlands and their proximity to Dresden

132

With Anna in Dresden

Bastei Bridge in Saxon Switzerland.

Photograph by Ahmad Ahmadov, Wikimedia Commons, 13 August 2016, CC-BY-4.0.
Rotated 2 degrees clockwise from the original and trimmed accordingly.

I also went to Zermatt, at the foot of the Matterhorn, and rode by cablecar to the top of the Klein Matternhorn. For more on this, refer back to my Maverick Traveller, which has a lot to say about mountaineering and goes into this in great detail.

One thing I thought was rather intolerant was the recent burqa ban and ban on the erection of mosques in Switzerland. Obviously the Swiss have decided that it is OK to hold meetings in Christian churches, but not in mosques, as it would seem.

Switzerland was nice, but I got over it quickly and decided that I was ready to move onward! What else was in store for me?

Next stop, Spain!

Geneva, where elections were being held

Geneva, with the Jet d'Eau and the Brunswick Monument, a Mausoleum build in 1879

Geneva: parkland and faux *beach*

Geneva: Outside the Palace of Nations. The Broken Chair monument
expressed opposition to land mines and cluster bombs.

CHAPTER SIX

Spain – First Glimpses of the Camino

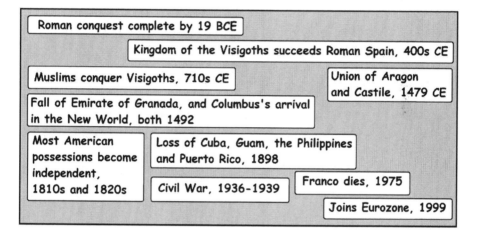

M Y intention has always been to get as much of the Camino de Europa under my feet as I can in this lifetime. Spain was the key to the doorway that stored a vast number of pilgrim sites and pathways within its borders. However, there are not just pilgrim sights in Spain, and I wanted to spend time learning about the people, Spanish culture and also just do a few laid-back touristy things.

I met so many interesting people while I was in Barcelona. I met a Jewish couple called Alexei and Sophia. They told me that they had wanted to get out of Russia as they were worried about their human rights if they stayed. Sophia had Spanish citizenship by this stage, while Alexei, who was an actor, was in Spain because he disagreed with the politics of Israel and didn't want to live in that country: which would otherwise have been a straightforward proposition.

I found that the public transport in Barcelona was excellent and trains and buses were easy to get on and off, though I was nearly molested by a taxi driver one night.

My first sights in Barcelona: the Plaça d'Espanya and the waterfront.

Bottom image by 'Canaan', Wikimedia Commons, taken on or before 28 April 2011, CC-BY-SA 4.0

You could see the beginnings of poverty in some areas of Barcelona. It was only just recently that the city elected a radical young woman in her early 40s – Ada Colau – to its mayoralty. Ms Colau is a long-time battler against housing evictions caused by unpayable mortgage debt. This is an example of the socialist and radical upsurge taking place in many parts of Europe right now.

Casa Batlló, interiors and roof decoration

Casa Milà, a hollow, helical building mainly designed by Gaudí, which is also nicknamed La Pedrera, 'the stone-quarry'

Casa Milà, a.k.a 'La Pedrera'

*Barcelona, including the Museu Nacional d'Art de Catalunya
with its cascading waterfalls*

*Barcelona: Parks,
Buildings and Gaudí*

Barcelona: Gaudí ceiling; beach; church architecture

Gaudí's Park Güell

Gaudi's Park Güell

La Sagrada Familia, by Gaudí

Casa Batlló, by Gaudí

Inside La Sagrada Familia

I learnt so much while I was there. Barcelona was a city built on the backs of Phoenicians and Carthaginians. It even has ties with the Greek god Hercules whose boat was lost in a storm and ended up in a place called 'Barca Nona', which is believed to be Barcelona today.

While I was in Barcelona I took a trip to the nearby Montserrat, which means 'serrated mountain' and which is the site of a famous Benedictine Abbey, in addition to being fascinating in itself.

Montserrat, which means the serrated mountain, like a saw. This mountain is about 35 km inland from downtown Barcelona, and also lends its name to the Caribbean island of Montserrat.

Montserrat with the Black Virgin of the Monastery

Spanish history is so rich and complex, with autonomous and culturally distinct regions such as Galicia, the Basque country and Catalonia, and I am completely fascinated by it. It's one of the reasons I love going there. Its history is so readily available through art, historical sites and architecture. The religious history is just as complex and interesting, even beyond the St James's way.

Spain's national religion is Catholicism, which was spread through Spain by St Paul the Apostle between the first and third centuries CE. Major conversion happened when Spain was in the hands of the Visigoths (meaning Western Goths), yet another Germanic tribe who moved in when Rome moved out in the same way that the ancestors of the Anglo-Saxons moved to England, and the Franks into France. In contrast to England, however, neither France nor Spain would end up with a German-based

Hiking the trails on Montserrat. Close up, the 'teeth' of the 'saw' are curiously rounded.

The Iberian Peninsula in the time of Ferdinand and Isabella (ca. 1492).
Source: PCL

language in the long run. The Franks gave their name to France but were eventually submerged in a Latin culture; and the Visigoths did not even succeed in giving their name to Spain, though they were very influential for a while.

Due to Christian Spain's proximity to Muslim (or Moorish) North Africa, there were many battles between the two and the taking and retaking of areas of Spain. The battle scars can still be seen, especially in Granada at the fortress of Alhambra, one place I fell in love with and felt really connected with. The crusades in the early part of the 1000s really began to shape Spain in terms of religion and it became an all-out war of Christians verses Muslims within the Iberian Peninsula. The Alhambra decree in the 1400s

155

required all persons residing within the Iberian Peninsula either convert to Christianity or get out...fast (whence, the Inquisition). Spain was also responsible for spreading Catholic Christianity to much of the 'New World' of Latin America and, in Asia, to the Philippines.

While I was in Barcelona, I didn't really have time to relax and take it all in. I was amazed by the sheer beauty of it all and I just loved the beaches. I met so many interesting people while I was in Barcelona. One couple I met gave me free passes to a whole lot of museums in Barcelona, so that was great.

However, there was one really frightening incident which I recall very clearly. I caught a taxi one day and the driver got all touchy feely on me and I knew he did not have good intentions. I told him that if he tried anything funky, he'd better watch the hell out. After that he drove to a suspect area of Barcelona and left me there. I made my way safely back into the city, though (thank God).

PAMPLONA

I was meant to take my leave of Spain after Barcelona and head to France, but I am a random traveller and I decided to get the train to Pamplona. I met a guy on Airbnb and stayed with him for a night. He told me he was growing marijuana in his lounge room and told me not to go in there. I let myself in anyway to have a look and told him he should really put a lock on it. He was supposed to be buying an apartment, but was unemployed. I did sympathise with him.

While I was in Spain I did learn a lot about what it was like to live there and it wasn't as flash as some people may think. Some of the locals have it quite tough. Spain has long had the harshest bankruptcy laws in Europe. Until 2003 individuals quite simply could not go bankrupt at all, and until

2015 individuals could not apply for bankruptcy themselves. Thus, creditors could earmark present and future earnings for all the money owing if they wanted to. That puts a lot of strain on families who have no money, no jobs, and debt that cannot be cancelled and simply keeps accruing interest as a consequence of economic depression and unstable housing markets. In wider economic terms, it is a recipe for a permanent economic depression that never ends and a culture in which nobody ever takes any kind of entrepreneurial risks of the sort that might get the economy going again.

It was a good idea to go to Pamplona. I could take a good look at what the trail was like and where it was heading before I did it properly. I find some people are fundamentalist about the pilgrim ways and needed to do the whole thing start to finish and clock up thousands of miles to feel justified in doing it. Not me, though. I was happy to do it in small parts, bit by bit.

I found Pamplona to be absolutely outstanding. I particularly loved eating in the local tavern where they had tapas. Where I was staying, I mingled more with the locals, buying food and eating out. It was a nice change, and not many tourists were around.

From Pamplona, I took the train to Toulouse, France. I loved the ride through the Pyrenees. I took regional train routes and boarded the train at the last station in Spain, Portbou, and crossed over into France.

CHAPTER SEVEN

France – When Pilgrims Took to the Mountains

The French Way of the Camino de Santiago

Roman conquest of Gaul completed, 52 BCE

Franks succeed Romans, late 400s CE. Franks give name to France, but are actually Germans. Modern French language mostly descended from Latin (Romans), not earlier Gaulish (Celtic) nor Frankish (German).

Large and strategically located, France becomes a dominant country in Europe for centuries. Many wars with England which long claimed French throne, symbolised by Unicorn in English/UK coats of arms. Last war with British ends at Battle of Waterloo after 1789 French Revolution, 1815.

Post-revolutionary France goes through two Empires, temporarily restored old-regime monarchy and five Republics; 5th Republic 1958-

Joins Eurozone, 1999

FRANCE is a country I have visited often. One of the happiest times I was there was for a reunion of former crew on the Chinese junk *La Dame de Canton*, now a floating restaurant on the Seine, in 2008. (I talk about my 1980s adventures on *La Dame de Canton* in *A Maverick Traveller*.) I have many friends in France, such as Jean-Claude, with whom I recently climbed Mont Blanc. I will have more to say about that, below.

France would be the beginning of my journey on the Camino del Norte – the Northern Way to Santiago. There are four main ways through France to Santiago de Compostela, The French Way being the most popular route. Then there is the Northern Way, the Le Puy Route, and the Paris Route. There are, of course, the other routes they call 'feeder routes' or alternative walks that eventually link up with the main walks. The farthest point north to begin in France is in Paris, although even then this route links up with one even further north in Amsterdam, so there really are endless routes one can chose to walk.

Over time I have walked a fair few of parts of these, beginning in Paris. I once lived in Paris for a few months solid, so I am well acquainted with the city. I loved Paris, and my exploration of the city lead me to walking long distances within it. Not the complete French Way, but a small part of it.

I arrived in Paris in August. I chose that time because I the last time I had been in Paris, in June, the tourists had been rife and you had to wait two hours to get into the Louvre, one of my favourite places in the world. I had sworn that there was just no way that I would be standing in a queue in June again. France at the time was suffering through the recession. There were huge levels of unemployment and a lot of homelessness in Paris. I had my iPhone stolen after just one month and that was certainly quite an experience.

*Chartres Cathedral under illumination (above);
Southeast View of Notre-Dame de Paris (below).*

Images Wikimedia Commons. Top picture by 'PtrQs', 27 September 2015, CC-
BY_SA 4.0. Bottom picture by 'Uoaei1', 10 October 2015, CC-BY-SA 4.0

*Vault of Notre-Dame de Paris and stained glass image of Jonah being
disgorged whole by the whale, in l'Église Saint-Aignan de Chartres.*

Images Wikimedia Commons. Top photograph by 'Uoae1', 10 October 2015, CC-BY-
SA 4.0. Bottom photograph by 'Reinhardhauke', 22 January 2011, CC-BY-SA 3.0.

My friend Jean-Claude lives in Breil-sur-Roya in southern France and he had invited me to stay with him. His home was a beautiful example of a thirteenth-century house, nestled right under the Alps by the Italian border. We spent some time around Casterino, an area that is filled to the brim with pilgrim trails. I thought Casterino was stunning and we did one of the day-walk trails through there. There are routes and pathways over much of France and over time I have walked through numerous different areas. Though I didn't do them in one go, I still like to think they count towards my lifetime pilgrim journey.

The Region of Mont Blanc, Lake Como, and Monte Viso

*Casterino, a tiny village in the Alpes-Maritimes,
the extreme south-eastern corner of France*

Breil-sur-Roya, a 'perched village' in the Alpes-Maritimes,
tightly overlooking the River Roya

*On the outskirts of Breil-sur-Roya. The tiny house in the bottom
photo was my favourite sight in the locality!*

MONT BLANC

One such walk that I believe counts towards my journey is my ascent of Mont Blanc with my good friend Jean-Claude. Mont Blanc is the highest point in Europe, peaking at 4,808 metres, and is no easy climb. It has one of the highest numbers of climbing deaths in the world, partly explained by the fact that it also gets a very large number of climbers of varying ability. We stayed in Chamonix in the foothills of the Graian Alps, the mountain range which includes Mont Blanc. Preparation meant spending seven days practising climbing to different heights to allow my body to adjust to the oxygen levels – called acclimatisation. Jean-Claude is a very experienced climber so I was really thankful that he had agreed to climb it with me. I am no stranger to mountaineering and have successfully climbed many mountains, including getting to base camp at Mt Everest (more about that in my book *A Maverick Himalayan Way*), but I still found it one of the most challenging.

I was climbing Mont Blanc a few months before I intended on starting the Camino de Santiago, and was probably crazy to bite off so many adventures at once. I can't help myself – I have an attraction to mountains and climbing them, the thrill of it alone is worthwhile.

The climb to the summit would be over a few days. The first day we caught a mountain rack-rail tram to Nid d'Aigle, a hut at 2,482 m, and then walked to the Tête Rousse hut. I met plenty of Kiwis and Australians there, which I found incredible. Like pilgrims, in a way, we were all there for one reason or another. It just amazes me the different reasons that motivate people to go to different places around the world that they feel a connection to.

The food in the huts was not wonderful, but the higher we climbed, the better it began to taste. Though, I think that when you are climbing all day, anything would taste a hundred times better than what it normally would.

The final hut we would stay before making our final ascent was the Refuge du Goûter. In an outdoors context, the word goûter usually means something like snack or packed lunch, so that Refuge du Goûter probably means something like 'lunchbox hut', though I will call it Goûter Hut. It was at the Goûter Hut that the realisation of what I was doing really hit home – the sunsets and scenery was out of this world. There are no words to describe it. Bitterly cold, everything is white and deep-blue tones, and then this stunning arrangement of colours paint the sky at dawn.

We set out as part of a group of thirty. It was about the time we got to the Dôme du Goûter – a shoulder of Mont Blanc also known as Bosses Ridge, after two bumps additional to the Dôme called Les Bosses – that people in our group of thirty started to falter. Jean-Claude and I were allowed to continue on ahead of the others, as Jean-Claude held a French mountaineering certificate which was one rung below that of a fully qualified guide, and if it wasn't for his ingenious non-freezing packs of water worn close to the body which I describe in *A Maverick Traveller*, I don't think I would have made it either. The summit was amazing – you could see 360 degrees all around. I could literally see three countries from here: France, Switzerland, and Italy far into the distance.

There is a pilgrim trail called Tour du Mont Blanc, which follows around the foothills of Mont Blanc. The trail takes ten days and goes through neighbouring Italy and Switzerland. It travels over ancient Roman trade routes, giving a small insight into the hard journeys pilgrims and traders would take just to reach their destination. One of the key pilgrim spots is Les Contamines-Montjoie, a historical village I had visited on my way to climb Mont Blanc. There is also a chapel, the Notre Dame de la Gorge, which has been a pilgrim stop since the time of Ancient Rome.

Another key walking route runs from Chamonix in France to Zermatt in Switzerland, one I had trekked as part of my acclimatisation. It passes over ancient Roman trading routes – another piece of fascinating history. It is called the Walkers Haute Route and is a difficult walk which needs much planning. It is a ten- to twelve-day walk through rocky peaks, glaciers

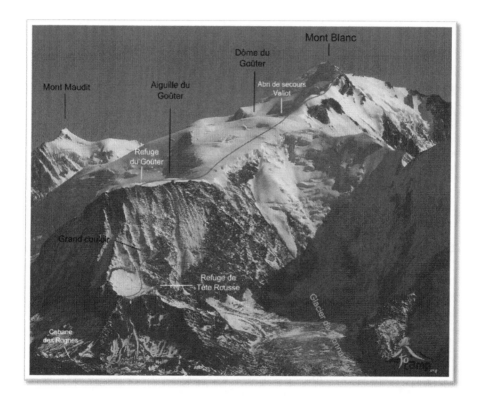

The Goûter Route up Mont Blanc.

Image by 'Christian' (June 2012), Wikimedia Commons, CC-BY-SA 2.0 France. Original posting is on URL https://www.camptocamp.org/ images/306760/fr/mont-blanc-voie-normale-par-le-gouter.

and high altitudes over 3,000 m. I didn't walk all of this – I rarely have the luxury of that much time – but even if I don't complete an entire walk, I at least attempt some part of it. It is a very popular walk and in the summer months you will often come across other walkers. I did end up travelling by bus from Chamonix to Zermatt after climbing Mont Blanc.

An early start for the final day

Acclimatisation

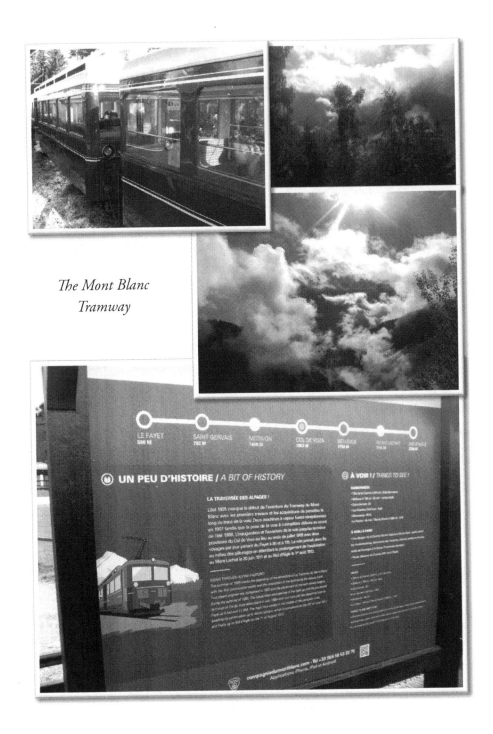

The Mont Blanc Tramway

Acclimatisation terrain

Mont Blanc and the Rocky Landscape at the top of the Tramway

On the ascent

Up and up

Têtr Rousse Hut at Sunset, and the next day ...

Reaching the famous Goûter Hut

With Jean-Claude at the very top of Mont Blanc!

The Mont Blanc Tram Tunnel

I did it! (Rules for Ascent of Mont Blanc.)

Chamonix

Getting ready to acclimatise to the mountains with Jean-Claude

Mont Blanc ice

LOURDES

I found France to be a treasure trove of history and it has some fine examples of Christian history. I had travelled to Lourdes in the south before beginning my walk to Santiago. This really impressed on me the dedication people have toward their religions, and even then, not everyone who was there was Catholic or even religious. While I was in Lourdes, I stayed in a neat place through Airbnb. I sat in on a few outdoor sermons and visited the Sanctuaires Notre-Dame de Lourdes, or the Domain, a major pilgrim site. I saw the famous healing springs, the Grotto of Massabielle, that are said to have sprung up from the ground after the Virgin Mary (Our Lady of Lourdes) appeared there in 1858.

There is a direct pilgrim trail from Lourdes to Santiago de Compostela, and the significance is no surprise.

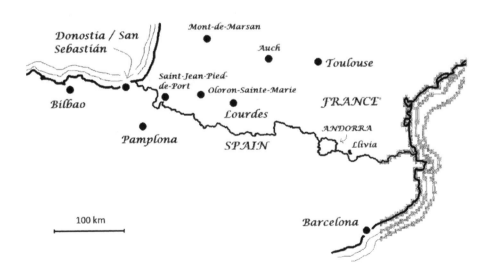

Lourdes, in relation to nearby towns on the French Way
and the wider region of the Pyrenees

Lourdes: the Basilica of our Lady of the Rosary

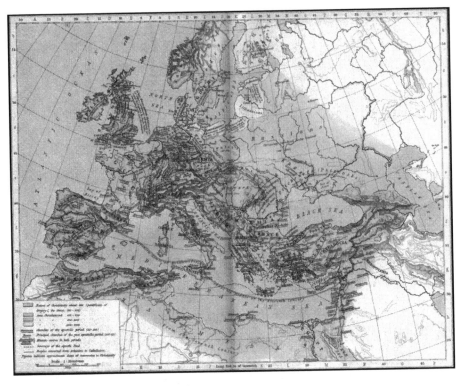

The Christianisation of Europe. Source: PCL.

The first written evidence of Christianity in France was from around the second century CE. This eventually led to the conversion of one of the founding rulers of France, Clovis I, referred to as the Father of France. Since then, there have been many important French religious figures emerge like Joan of Arc. France has a strategic position and the very first written records come from when the Romans ruled the country, known then as Gaul.

LYON AND MARSEILLE

The cities of Lyon and Marseille are key places to visit for pilgrims. They were tied very closely with the beginnings of Christianity in France, and both areas are inundated with sacred sites. I had done a quick trip to Lyon and I remember being inundated with historical information.

I saw the Amphitheatre of Three Gauls there, a great piece of outdoor architecture dating back to 9 CE. It is part of a complex called the Sanctuary of Three Gauls which acted as a religious and political arena for three new Gallic provinces that had just been added to the Roman Empire: Gallia Aquitania, Gallia Belgica and Gallia Lugdunensis, named after the city of Lugdunum, modern-day Lyon. Divided by the Romans into several provinces, Gaul was an area in the western part of Europe where Celtic tribes resided. Though most of Gaul occupied the area that is now France, the provinces of Gaul spilled over into Belgium and northern Italy as well.

CORSICA

Another area I had visited that is considered a pilgrim site is the large island of Corsica, which lies to the south of France in an otherwise Italian part of the Mediterranean Sea and which is shown, for convenience, in a map at the beginning of Chapter Ten (Italy). The French colonised the island over two centuries ago, and the entire cultural feel is really different from the French mainland. Napoleon Bonaparte was born here, making the island a popular destination not just for pilgrims. I did a few walks and treks around Corsica (Corse in French) in an area called Bonifacio that overlooks the Mediterranean Sea and is full of beautiful hills and forestry. I was actually surprised at the number of different hikes and walks throughout Corsica – 40% of the island is made up of forests and national parks. There was one day we couldn't go out for a walk because it was considered too dangerous as it was the local hunting day and all the people of Corsica seemed to be out with their guns and dogs.

One of the main trails leads right through the centre of the island and stops at some of the religious pilgrim sites along the way. Many of these were inland and high in the granite rock hillsides. There are a number of sacred sites on Corsica, like the Church of Santa di U Niolu, which is home to a well-known statue of St Mary. It was built in commemoration of a ship in the 15th century which found its way safely to the island of Corsica in a storm after an apparition of Mary showed them the way.

I went back to Lourdes for a few nights to nut out my journey and make a few final decisions on different aspects of the trip. As I had made my way through France, I had noted the different terrains and transport options in the different areas. I had thoroughly planned and researched the many different ways throughout France and Spain before finally settling on one: the Camino del Norte – the Northern Way.

CHAPTER EIGHT

Camping on the Camino del Norte

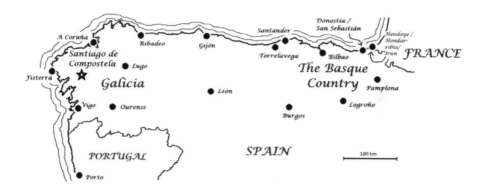

The Camino del Norte or Northern Way runs mainly along the northern coast of Spain, from Hendaye in France westward to Ribadeo, before turning inland to Santiago de Compostela

T HERE are so many pilgrim trails leading to Santiago de Compostela: the Northern Way, the Primitive Way, the Inland Way, the Baztanés Way, the Lebaniego Way and the French Way. It surprised when me I started researching all the different 'Ways' how many there actually were. I had already made plans to walk the Northern Way, the Camino del Norte. Since I have travelled on the Camino del Norte, I have learnt that there is now a mobile app that pilgrims can use to get relevant information when on the Camino ways – how incredible! I have included this in a list of useful websites at the end of the book. Modern technology mingling with

189

something so ancient and old – great! I might have to download it and use it the next time I get myself there to finish off my journey! On any of the routes, pilgrims receive a *credencial*, a pilgrim passport that you get stamped at different places along the way just so you can prove you did reach them to receive your certificate at the end – proof that you were there.

The definition of a pilgrimage is simply to travel to a sacred place. The routes give modern-day pilgrims the chance for reflection, penance for sins and the chance to meet other travellers. Pilgrimages are quite a social activity and you don't have to be religious to undertake one. I had toyed with the idea of doing such a trek for most of my life, and as I was making my way over the Camino de Europa, going all the way to Santiago would be the icing on the cake. I am more of a hiker than a rock climber, that's for sure.

I truly believe the best part of travelling is meeting people; locals or other tourists. So, I decided that's exactly what I was going to do. I had a bit of space in my busy schedule so I made plans to walk the Camino to Santiago. I knew before I started that I wasn't going to be able to do the whole walk at once. We always find reasons not to do things, to travel, to walk, to trek and to go on pilgrimages. We do live busy lives, but I knew I could find the time, and if not, I would simply make it.

I knew the feeling at the end would be indescribable, and although I knew I couldn't do the whole 'Way' at once, I was at least going to do part of it and make a start. This would be my journey, the journey of my lifetime. And hey, if I'm 70 years old when I finish, I can at least say I did it; I made it to the end of the Camino at Santiago. I think it's better than sitting and saying, well, I wish I had done that. So, I decided I was going to walk the Northern Way to Santiago, the less-travelled of the Ways. The walk would have taken me over a month to complete if I walked it all the way and did it all at once. On this trip, I planned to spend roughly a week: a solid 7–8 days of walking in my leather boots and with my tent on my back.

My journey began at Hendaye in the south of France, right on the border with Spain. It lies just beyond the foothills of the Pyrenees mountain ranges, which means walking through the ranges along the Via Agrippa, an ancient Roman road built by Marcus Vipsanius Agrippa, which takes you into Spanish country. It eventually links up with the main route, the French Way, at Arzua. It also combines with parts of the Coastal Way.

Hendaye, known to the Basques as Hendaia, was a brilliant little seaside town and you could start to see more signs of pilgrims here. In a square in the centre of town stood the exquisite Great Cross of Hendaye, which is one of the many relics honouring Christianity as an important part of French history and another site for pilgrims. There were plenty of pilgrim hostels here, but I had got off the train at a reasonable hour and had decided to make a start on crossing the foothills of the Pyrenees.

This part of the crossing wasn't going to be overly difficult; the main difficulty was adjusting to walking all day with a heavy backpack. I wasn't sure how far I could get with all my stuff in it from the last few months of travelling around I had done.

A few hours later I found myself in Irun, my first taste of Spain on the Camino. I was really taken with Irun. Irun is a small coastal town, sitting pretty much on the water's edge opposite Hendaye. Irun was the focal point of the Romanisation of the Basque country and has always been a point of reference for pilgrims making the journey as far back as the ninth century.

In Irun, the parish church Nuestra Señora del Juncal is a key place for pilgrims to visit. Since the ninth century, pilgrims have the tradition of stopping here to worship and pray before continuing on their way. It was a tradition, if not a right, that pilgrims stopped at all, if not some, of the

Hendaia (Hendaye) on the distant, French side of the river Bidasoa,
Hondarrabia and Irun on the near side of the river (Spain).

Photograph by Joxemai, 31 October 2016, Wikimedia Commons, CC-BY-SA 4.0

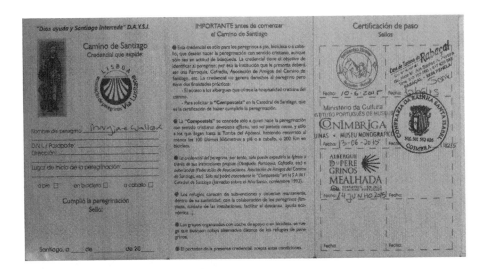

The Pilgrim Passport

(some personal information deleted)

little churches or *ermitas* all along the Way. There were evening prayers, and outdoor and indoor prayers that travellers could sit in on or listen to. I did like the Nuestra Señora del Juncal – it was lovely.

It was at this point I remember feeling like I was going a bit mad because my pack felt really heavy. I had my tent in it and it was the Spanish summer, so it was really warm. I had also made the mistake of leaving my summer tramping boots with my friend in Cannes, so I was wearing my leather tramping boots, which was not ideal in the heat. Even now, I need to get myself a bit more sorted and get four-season tramping boots suited to all weather. Not leather!

For most of the Northern Way you are walking on concrete. I remember reading a blog about just how concreted it was. Walking on concrete was actually harder than anything I had ever done before. It was harder than walking in the Rockies or the Himalayas, to be honest. It was extremely difficult.

So, because my pack was so heavy, I decided I needed to get rid of some of it. I found a little post shop and I went inside and asked in English for a big box. I must have looked like some mad homeless woman. So, I was in this little Spanish post shop, putting everything that I thought I wouldn't need in this big box to post back home. I made a big mistake. I ended up putting my New Zealand passport into the box. I didn't realise at the time, though, so I went ahead and sellotaped it all up because I was in such a hurry to continue walking. There were three people behind the counter watching me. I could tell they thought I was mad, and one of them basically stated that I was mad. I know she did. I don't speak Spanish, but I could tell. I said, 'Look, I don't speak Spanish, but I can tell from the tone of your voice that you think I'm mad.' They looked at me, so I said, 'Well, I'm actually a pilgrim and I'm doing the Camino de Santiago and I want a light pack, if you don't mind.' I then told them I have done this all over the world. Later on, I was going to regret putting my New Zealand passport into that box.

When I returned to New Zealand and tried to enter the country, I didn't have a permit to do so, so I had to come into the country on a holiday permit on my British passport. Thank God, I didn't send that one as well. They asked me at the airport if I had a ticket to leave New Zealand again. Luckily, I did have a ticket I had booked from New Zealand to Japan, so I showed them that. That ticket to Japan was the only reason I was allowed in. I had to pay them $300 to have a lifetime free entry into New Zealand on my British passport, which I thought was quite hilarious. It was actually quite serious, though, as for about one week I couldn't receive any medical benefits and I couldn't work.

So, after I had posted my big box, I continued walking. I remember the beautiful coastline. I ended up meeting a young woman from Holland whose name was Maron. She was running an organic produce shop in the north of Holland. She came from an area of Holland that spoke a different language to the rest of the country. I think this was Frisian, a survival of Anglo-Saxon days and the nearest language in Continental Europe to English. Maron and I got on exceedingly well; we joked and we laughed together. We decided to walk together and stay in San Sebastián on our way. San Sebastián. Oh, what a beautiful city. San Sebastián is on the coast and I really loved it. San Sebastián is in the Bay of Biscay, and is a beautiful resort town with world-class restaurants. It was quite a sight, especially when you have been walking for so long. It is quite a popular place for tourists, and I could see why. I felt like I was just saying wow the entire time!

In the past, this area was ruled by the Romans, and then became part of the Kingdom of Navarre (earlier, the Kingdom of Pamplona) that had lands in Spain and France. Navarre was a Basque state, which was gradually incorporated into Spain and France in a similar fashion to the way that Scotland was incorporated into the United Kingdom; even today, Navarre maintains a shadowy constitutional existence, since the King of Spain is titled not only as the King of Spain but also the King of Navarre.

It was nice to have someone to walk with that I did get on with so well. I learnt a lot about Maron. I suppose it is all about the people you meet on your way. People trek for different reasons and the reasons they decide to do the pilgrim ways are all different. Maron had just got out of a seven-year

Two Views of Donostia / San Sebastián, by night and by day, both taken from the top of Mount Igeldo.

Both images Wikimedia Commons. Top photograph by **Валерий Дед** (Valerii Ded), 7 January 2017, CC-BY- 3.0. Bottom photograph by 'Keta', 26 July 2008, CC-BY-2.5

relationship with a man who had bipolar. It sounded dreadful. That was, I guess, part of the reason she was here trekking. We used to talk about men. One time I remember we were talking and I was honest about how old I was. She looked at me and basically said, 'Well, I don't want to end up like you.' I said, 'Well, at least I am single, happy and free. I'm not bogged down by unhealthy relationships and have the freedom to do things on my own.'

A piece of church artwork that caught my eye

The Camino de Santiago in the misty Basque Country

*Pilgrim Churches and some
time off in San Sebastián*

It was interesting, you know, you could tell the pilgrims from tourists. The pilgrims looked rough and ready and exhausted, the tourists didn't. Anyway, we found a commune to spend the night in. It was run by a religious group called the Twelve Tribes of Israel. We only had to pay a donation to stay there. They had a very ordered society based on the biblical testaments. The commune had been established in the 1970s and they were all about being self-sufficient and ran many different establishments all over the world. The food they produced was amazing. They had their own bakery, their own organic farm and they had their own organic vegetables. The accommodation was glorious too, and I would most definitely stay there again. The fact that there was no drinking or smoking allowed certainly did not put me off, either.

Anyway, we stayed here for one night and it was just beautiful. The commune ran an organic shop in San Sebastian, which we went to see. I remember the tofu. I don't really eat tofu, but I tried their sundried tomato and olive tofu and couldn't help but love it. It was delicious. Oh, and they had a Danish bread there too– wow, nirvana! I'm sorry, their food was just beyond words – it really was. They did try and convert us, though. I told them that nobody could convert me.

They ran a home-school centre in their German commune. In Germany, the media had picked on them and they had been ostracised there. I never did get to the bottom of it. I do agree that such communes require rules that they all need to abide by. I did admire that about them. I also noticed that they took on a lot of men who couldn't live their lives by themselves and who were alcoholics. And I thought, well, I have no issues with that. I suppose they were just trying to help and maybe it would work for them.

Anyway, after we had left San Sebastián, Maron and I just chatted too much and sat around drinking cups of tea. I quite liked having the company and we did get on really well. One day she said to me that she wanted to forge on ahead and that she didn't want to trek with me anymore. I thought it was funny, though I suppose we did do a lot of talking and drinking tea. So, I thought, okay, fair enough, that was her choice, we'd got rather behind in our schedule. Unlike me, Maron was doing the entire Camino right there and then. I knew I had a time limit on my journey. So, we decided to at least get ourselves to the next town and then say our goodbyes there. One minute we were in the beautiful boutique suburbs of San Sebastián, the next we were the pilgrim walkers headed off into the distance.

We were headed to Zarautz and we hadn't booked any accommodation there. We got caught in torrential rain on the way. We eventually found some accommodation after we were completely saturated. In Zarautz, Maron left and carried on her way. I suppose time was moving on, so she went and did her own thing, and I did mine. I walked through the villages of Getaria, Zumaia and Deba. It was great; there were beautiful churches everywhere and I loved walking along the coast line. I walked amidst lush fields past the famous town of Gernika-Lumo. Gernika, known in Spanish as Guernica, and now joined to neighbouring Lumo, is the town so notoriously bombed in 1937: an episode commemorated in Picasso's famous painting. Even before then, it was a town of great historical significance to the Basques, the site of a famous oak tree symbolising their freedoms and their identity.

Water was a godsend. I found a renewed appreciation of water in general. It was particularly hot, and I did struggle a bit with the heat – although this far into the Camino I had become slightly used to it. You always felt hot and sticky and I had got to the point I just didn't care what I looked like too much – I didn't care if my hair was sticking up from the heat or it was stuck to my head – the dreaded 'hat hair'.

I believe I got as far as Arratzu, near Bilbao, and that's a funny story in itself. I was getting quite tired at this stage and met a young guy who was with an older Russian woman who was all over him. He was an Australian who was getting sponsorship to complete the trail. I've become quite suspicious of people who require sponsorship now, as it is often a fiddle. He asked me if I'd sponsor him, if I was excited and if I was going to finish the whole way to Santiago de Compostela. There is a bit of pilgrim snobbery in the sense that people are always worried about where you started and how long you have walked and whether or not you are walking it all at once or in stages. I told him that this wasn't my first walk, I was experienced and that I was tired. I told him about what I had done and where I had been and his mouth just dropped open. He did say to me that I had every right to be tired. I thought, well, you know, I do have every right to be tired. I *was* tired – one week was enough of that type of trekking.

It was more about the people I met while walking. I met people from all over and made friends like Maron. A lot of people I met were in their 60s. You hear of people trekking in their 70s and I think, well, good on them. You do need to be an experienced trekker, though. You don't just go to Spain and expect to walk the whole length of any of the Ways. It is tough going and a lot of people just turn up and expect to do it, a lot in their late 70s. If you're not experienced and it's not something your body is used to, really, why would you do it to yourself? I mean, you'd have been better off doing it when you were a bit younger.

Anyway, while I was in Arratzu I met a lovely girl from Madrid, a couple from Madrid, and a girl from the south of Spain. We were all doing the Northern Way and formed a group to walk together. It was funny, though, I was the only non-Spanish speaking person and they proceeded to take it upon themselves to look after me. They arranged for us all to stay in a nice apartment while we were in Arratzu, and we stayed for two nights in a row.

The arrangement was great because they all spoke Spanish and we didn't have to stay in any of the pilgrim hostels. They went out and they negotiated meals, and for $10 we had paella and so much food – anything and everything – you name it, we had it. So, the food got better and the

Paella with Friends

accommodation got better. I really enjoyed it because I got to mix more with the local people and not just the overseas tourists.

The Camino was hard yakka. The thing I loved most was the people and the camaradrie. It made me want to do a trail closer to home next.

Maron got in touch with me later on and told me she had made it to the end, to Santiago del Compostela. I'm now friends with her on Facebook and she got hold of me last October asking me if I wanted to do the El Camino with her and to continue where I left off. I said no, though. I didn't have the time then, but I will arrange to do it with her another time and continue with it.

I suppose, in a way, I'm in no rush. I live in a beautiful country called New Zealand, I'm still fit and I have the rest of my life in which to finish it.

CHAPTER NINE

The Caminho Português

> Early history similar to Spain but Muslim rule ends earlier, in 1249. Boundaries of Portugal established in 1200s and have hardly changed since. Alliance with England (1386) is world's oldest treaty still in effect.
>
> Early period of heroic exploration in the 1400s (Henry the Navigator). Creation of Portuguese Empire follows.
>
> Union with Spain, 1581-1668. Initially amicable, this union ended in a lengthy Portuguese war of independence.
>
> Catastrophic earthquake of 1755 is followed by extensive and grand rebuilding under Marquis of Pombal, the 'Pombaline' era
>
> Twentieth century witnesses First Republic, semi-fascist dictatorship 1926-1974, 'Carnation Revolution' 1974, and joining of Eurozone in 1999

THE Caminho Português de Santiago, or Camino Portugués in Spanish, is a series of walks that lead you to Santiago de Compostela from origins in Portugal. There are a number that begin in different areas of Portugal. These routes are more rural than the standard routes used to get there through Spain and give the traveller a different cultural experience altogether.

Portugal – what a fabulous place. The name Portugal was formed from 'Portus Cale', the name given to the area by the ancient Romans. As I have found when travelling through it, Portugal was largely influenced by the Romans and has some really good ruins which are worth seeing. The landscape varies between mountainous ranges, thick forestry and low-lying coastal areas. I had always heard how beautiful Portugal was and that was the main reason I had wanted to go there originally. The total population of Portugal sits at around 10.5 million, with Lisbon the largest city, followed by Porto.

I arrived in Lisbon and stayed in a beautiful old hostel that was listed on Airbnb. I stayed for two nights and fell completely in love with the city. There was so much going on, and everywhere I looked there were beautiful old buildings. Lisbon is on the coast and I'd heard it had great beaches as well as the wide River Tagus running through the city.

I arrived in the middle of June, which was Portugal's summer. It was scorching, and I found it very hot. There were festivals being held everywhere, and outdoor bands playing in the main streets. The smell of fried sardines was in the air – something I thought was actually really weird. The Portuguese seem to love frying sardines. They have a street party or a festival – they fry sardines. I later found out it was the Feast of St Anthony (or, the festival of sardines!) held in mid-June every year and includes the tradition of frying sardines everywhere.

What really surprised me was that Portugal was 70% dependent on renewable energy. They had built all these incredible renewable energy sources, way more even than Germany. I think it's the world's best-kept secret. Portugal was one of the 'PIGS', short for 'Portugal, Ireland, Greece, Spain', an economic term in the EU that meant that they were on the verge of economic collapse. There were changes being suggested that would kill off their public health system and many people were opposing that. But I would love to go back, as I did enjoy it. I also learnt that many English people are buying up property in Portugal.

I found people were always heading to the beach. Portugal has some great surf beaches, and though I'm not really a surfer, it is something I would have liked to do while I was there. One thing I noticed was there didn't seem to be many migrants in Portugal. I did notice that there were a lot of roaming dogs about and people had warned me to be wary of drinking the water in the outskirts of Lisbon.

I visited a few art galleries there and spent most of my time out sightseeing. I also went to the Santa Casa de Misericórdia, a 15th-century charity that was founded by Queen Leonor of Portugal. Around Lisbon the streets are paved and narrow with townhouses and buildings lining the streets. There were plenty of old churches that I visited there as well.

Lisbon Church Interior

Lisbon

Lisbon street scene, with a curious ceremonial gate at the end of the street. It looks like there is a park beyond. But it is all very mysterious.

Triumphal Arch in Rua Augusta, Lisbon, fronting onto the Praça do Comércio.

Photograph by Diego Delso, 12 May 2012, Wikimedia Commons, CC-BY-SA 3.0

*The Igreja de Carmo ('blue tile church') and adjacent
convent, and another impressive building in Lisbon*

Why the Igreja de Carmo is called the 'blue tile church'

Another charming building, one of a great many

Even though I loved the city, I was desperate to get out into the countryside to the less touristy areas of Portugal.

There was a network of pilgrim ways through Portugal to Santiago de Compostela. I did a YouTube investigation of the Caminho Português which showed the routes and their characteristics. As I really didn't want to walk on a concrete highway, I decided that I would do a combination, sticking to unsealed trails. I wanted to see the less popular and less touristy areas and get to know the real Portugal. I would walk parts and also take the bus at times because of time limitations. The scenery was pleasant and it passed through vineyards, past farms and through quaint rural villages. At times, it was quite hard to find which way to go and I ended up taking a few wrong turns.

One of the first places I stopped at on the way was Santarém. I took a bus and train there from Lisbon and on arrival found it was a very ancient, beautiful and incredible city. The city had been founded by the Romans in second century BCE and there are still Roman roads here. The city is rich with historical and religious sites like the Cabaças Tower and many churches from medieval times. Santarém is the site of a Eucharistic miracle from the 13th century, which after investigation from the Catholic Church, was approved as a miracle. The legend said that a woman sought help with the infidelity of her husband and was given a piece of bread which began to bleed. It was then mysteriously captured in a crystal pyx (container for the Eucharist bread) and it still remains like that to this day. You can find it in the Church of the Holy Miracle. I spent one night in Santarém and really enjoyed my time there.

There are many shrines around Portugal, the most famous being the Shrine of Our Lady of Fátima, not far from Santarém. They really are dedicated to their faith. So, it was to Fátima that I headed next, an almost

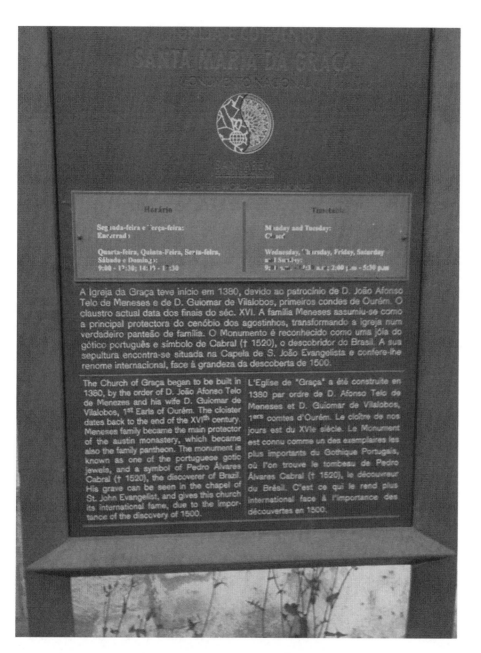

Santarém: Santa Maria da Graça

Santarém

Santarém

eleven-hour walk north of Santarém. Fátima was quite beautiful, and I noted that it was not as touristy as Lourdes. As I had been to Lourdes before and visited a similar pilgrim site there, I really wanted to see the Lady of Fátima shrine.

Fátima is another prominent place for Catholics. In 1917, some young children saw an apparition of a beautiful lady, the Virgin Mary, who is also referred to as Our Lady of Fátima or Our Lady of the Rosary. Our Lady of Fátima foretold miracles to the three children. Around 70,000 people claimed to witness one of the miracles in 1917 when the sun appeared to dance before the crowds. In the area that Our Lady of Fátima appeared, the Cova di Iria, a spring appeared which is said to heal people even now in modern times. In 1932, the Catholic Church approved the miracle and Our Lady of Fátima, making it a very important place for Catholics and Christians.

Among the other important pilgrimage sites in Portugal are the Bom Jesus do Monte in Braga and Nossa Senhora dos Remédios in Lamego.

From Fátima, I decided that my next destination was Tomar. I got severely lost on my way there and was really frustrated at the lack of signs. I couldn't even find a bus. However, I thought it was truly the most beautiful place. I met a couple there, an American lady and her friend, a local Portuguese man. She was walking the Camino de Portuguese and was covering 35 kilometres a day, which was really quite good considering it was on concrete. She hated it and was telling me about the dramas she had had walking on concrete. Although it was hard, she had given herself 30 days to complete it and was going to do so, come hell or high water.

Tomar is another really nice town in Portugal with old buildings and churches everywhere. I loved a beautiful square they had in the centre of town called Convento da Ordem de Cristo. There was an old church that sat

Fátima

at one end of it and a monument in the centre; it was a cool place to hang out in. Tomar's history involved the Knights Templar with the Convent of Christ, which was their 15th-century stronghold. The Knights Templar was a medieval branch of Christianity officially endorsed by the Catholic Church in the early 1100s. Their official role was to protect pilgrims who were making their pilgrimages through Europe. Their existence came about by the loss of the Holy Land and the loss of pilgrim sites and paths there. Highwaymen purposely sought out pilgrims to rob them and murdered

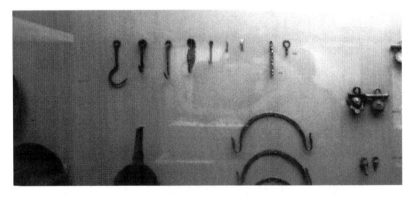

Modern-looking Roman kitchen hardware,
from the excavations near Coimbra

The countryside near the Coimbra excavations

many on their journeys, and so the Knights Templar came about as a means of protection. From the 13ᵗʰ century onwards, their numbers fell into decline and they spread further afield to places like Tomar on the Iberian Peninsula until the group was closed down and their strongholds turned into convents and monasteries.

*Coimbra: the church
Carlos worked at*

Coimbra: Claustro da Sé Velha (Cloister of the Old Cathedral) above; Church of São Tiago (St. James) below. Both fundamentally predate the invention of Gothic architecture and its soaring vaults and pointed arches in the 1200s CE.

Pilgrim Picnic Area near Coimbra

Coimbra: Rustic Scenes

Coimbra Street Scene

Cross, artwork and Roman Ruins around Coimbra

Roman Ruins near Coimbra

Museum at the Coimbra Roman Excavations

I ended up in Coimbra, the ancient Roman capital of Portugal. It was known as Aeminium in Roman times and has many well-preserved archaeological remains. It is home to the best-preserved church in Portugal from this era: The Old Cathedral, Sé Velha. Coimbra sits on the Mondego River and is home to the best university in the country, so it's full of students. I found the beautiful Monastery of Santa Cruz, which has a lavishly decorated exterior. There were two tall towers outside topped with many crosses: a very stunning building.

I met a few local guys and we sat around talking and drinking beer. One of the guys, Carlos, managed a commune. He managed the church and his father was a member of the church too. Here I was, sitting with someone who was 27 years old with a master's degree and with zero opportunities for him to get work. Another guy was in his 30s and still waiting to have a life.

I also visited a museum: the Museu Nacional Machado de Castro. I walked around for two hours and my mouth was wide open the whole time. Among the artefacts, I saw modern-looking kitchen hardware that the Romans used when they occupied the area. The ruins over which the museum is built, a Roman forum, were the best I'd ever seen in all of Europe. I got talking with the guard at the gate and told him how incredible I thought it was. He told me that Portugal didn't have enough money to excavate any more of the ruins and that there were more under the museum than were in it. I told him they seriously needed to consider getting funding because people should be able to see such incredible pieces of history.

In Coimbra, I also found the Monastery St Clare, or, the Monastery of Santa Clara-a-Nova. It has now been turned into a church dedicated to the St Queen Elizabeth, or Isabel of Aragon as she is otherwise known. While I was visiting the church, I met Cristovão, the museum's curator. He is a very

Porto: Avenida de Montevideu

Porto: the trees that look so much like New Zealand Pohutukawa, and the fort of São Francisco do Queijo

interesting person and we became fast friends. He's one of my Facebook friends now.

I took a bus up to Porto and stayed there for a few nights. I felt relieved at getting back to the coast and the sea breezes. Porto is the second-largest city with around 500,000 people residing there and is very grand.

I spent a lot of time on the main street that runs alongside the Duoro River, south of the main city and port. There were some beautiful parks here like the Pérgola da Foz, and I noticed trees around that looked very similar to the New Zealand Pohutukawa trees, of which at least a couple of old specimens are known to be planted in Lisbon, and one in the city known in Galician as A Coruña (La Coruña in Castilian Spanish), in Galicia. Maybe these were some other ones. I took a bus around Porto and visited a few art galleries here, which were all really interesting. The bus route went alongside the river and past ruins sitting on clifftops. There were some that sat right in among modern buildings and houses. I saw the ruins of the Fort of São Francisco do Queijo (otherwise known as the Castle of Cheese!). It was quite a contrast of old and new, but I think most of Portugal is like that.

CHAPTER TEN
Italy – The Home of the Stone King, the Pope and €1 Coffees

Italy

This map also includes Corsica and identifies the
location of Bonifacio in Corsica, see Chapter 7.

229

Roman Empire: Italy at the heart till Western Empire falls (476 CE), decays thereafter. City of Rome depopulates from one million to only twenty or thirty thousand for many centuries to come.

Italy revives in the Middle Ages. Social structure dominated by independent city-states, not feudal castles in the countryside.

A more progressive, less feudal social structure means the Renaissance happens first in Italy.

Italy is politically re-unified as an independent nation, for the first time since ancient times, in 1871 (the *Risorgimento,* the 'Resurgence')

Performance of Italian central government proves disappointing. The South, isolated on the end of a long peninsula, remains stubbornly underdeveloped.

Fascist dictatorship, then economic advance after WWII. Eurozone, 1999.

I love Italy and the ancient Romans– what a powerful group of people! The churches, the art, sculptures and ancient ruins just make Italy a wonderful place to visit on a pilgrimage. That is, Italy and pilgrimages just go hand in hand, don't they? For most people, Italy conjures up ideas of the Vatican, coffee, wine, vineyards, stunning architecture and religion. Religion has always been influential in Italy – Christianity wasn't always so popular. Before it became the state religion, Christians were persecuted and fed to lions as entertainment in the Roman stadiums! Well, what a turnaround. In 313 CE, Emperor Constantine adopted Christianity as his faith and issued the Edict of Milan so the citizens could decide whether the country should adopt Christianity as its state religion. Well, he succeeded because ten years later, it was! The Romans went from one end of the scale to the other over a few hundred years with the very first church built in Judea during the time that it was a province of the Roman Empire. Of course, Italy was going to be an important part of my Camino.

The coffee in Italy was one thing I thoroughly enjoyed – coffees only cost €1 and were delicious: rich, aromatic and full of flavour. I found it is quite cheap to live in Italy: the price of food is pretty good compared to other European countries.

VATICAN CITY

I had visited the Vatican while I was doing my Eurobus trip in the 1990s, and it was then that I really got a sense of the full extent of the Roman Empire, since Rome was so far from Britain! I also realised that the Romans had never conquered the Scottish Highlands, like I had once thought they had.

At the foothills of the Grampian Mountains in Scotland is the site of a fierce battle which took place between the Romans and Caledonians, or Scots, numbering some 30,000 soldiers. The Caledonians were defeated, but the Romans didn't attempt to further invade Caledonia.

The Roman Empire in the first Century CE. Source: PCL.

231

Instead, the Romans built a wall – Hadrian's Wall – to keep the wild Highlanders out! In the first century CE, the Roman Empire already controlled much of the south of the island of Great Britain, that is to say the area that would later become England and Wales, and this came to be seen as enough. They never really bothered with Ireland either.

Italy's history lies in the ancient ruins found throughout the country as well as in all the others they ruled during their Roman heyday. They ruled Britain, parts of Europe, Turkey and basically everywhere around the Mediterranean. Christianity was a major part of Roman history, first introduced by the apostles.

Rome has several sites where some of the twelve apostles are reportedly buried. Saints Peter and Paul were known to have spent time around Italy preaching the gospel. Many relics from the apostles are also found in Italy, of which the majority lie within the Vatican. When you look back through the medieval era you can see the supreme influence the popes had over societies, including their monarchs.

While I was in the Vatican City I visited St Peter's Basilica, the biggest of its kind in the world. St Peter's remains are encased in a tomb directly beneath the high altar and it has become a commonplace to visit for pilgrims from all over the world. The exterior is a fine example of the stunning Italian Renaissance architecture with elaborately decorated facades and an interior that makes your mouth drop open. I was really blown away with the lavishness of everything, nothing was held back, and I admired the Romans with their taste for decoration and architectural style.

I learnt so much about the Vatican and its role in the development and conversion of nations to the Catholic faith. The area the Vatican sits on has always been considered sacred to the Romans and was the site of a shrine to an ancient Roman goddess. The Vatican was established as the headquarters for Catholicism around the time the Old St Peter's Basilica was built around the fourth century. It is proof of the influences of Christianity over the development of countries and establishment of monarchs. Countries that claimed Catholicism as their state religion looked to the Vatican for approval, guidance and, most importantly, funding. The Vatican is one of the main pilgrimage sites in the world, and its popularity was evident when I visited – there were tourists everywhere. I remember walking around among mass crowds of other tourists and pilgrims who were all there for different reasons. I loved how massive it was and the feeling of being there – something so old and yet new was just so humbling. The Vatican was one of the most powerful religious influences from the day it was built until even now. The Pope never ceases to gather massive crowds to hear his speeches even today. In the past, the Pope ruled over various Papal States as a secular ruler, in addition to ruling the Catholic church. In 1870 Italy became unified and the papacy retreated to the Vatican, which was now part of Italy. It was only in 1929 after signing the Lateran Pact with the Italian regime of Benito Mussolini that the Vatican once more became a state independent in its own right.

While I was in the Vatican City in 1996, I learnt that a good friend of mine had suddenly passed away. It was completely unexpected and that dampened my memories of that initial visit. (I talk about this in *A Maverick Traveller*.)

There is an Italian camino that runs from Vatican City and connects up with other trails that lead to Santiago de Compostela. It is a huge journey, and I am quite proud of the fact that I have done parts of it over the years. The main walks I did through Italy were through the Monte Viso that borders Italy and France, a part of the Via Francigena, and some of the trails around Milan.

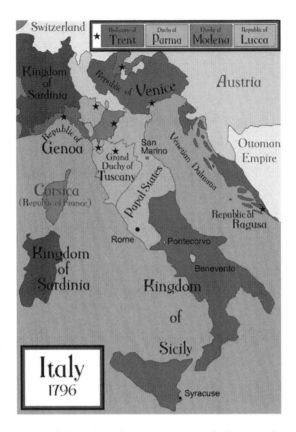

*The political dvisions of Italy sometime before unification,
showing the Papal States.*

Source: 'Capmo', 21 April 2009, in the Wikipedia entry on the Papal
Statess, CC-BY- SA 3.0 (rendered monochrome for this book).

VENICE

I went to Venice as well during my 1990s Eurobus trip; another stunning
example of the Italian Renaissance. I visited some of the little islands around
Venice which are only a short ferry ride into the beautiful Adriatic Sea.
There were hundreds of them all sitting in the ocean across from Venice.
I spent three days wandering around and visiting some of the churches,

the art galleries and just enjoying the holiday vibes. Venice was once an independent republic – officially the Most Serene Republic of Venice. It was founded in the seventh century and abolished by invading French revolutionaries in 1797. The French did a lot of abolishing in this era. Along with the French Monarchy, Venice and the Holy Roman Empire, the revolutionaries and Napoleon also abolished the Spanish Inquisition and its Italian offshoot, not before time.

There was so much detail in some of the buildings which was really was a high note for me. There were carved facades with gold detail that shone brightly in the sun.

Leonardo da Vinci is one of my favourite artists, and I think he is just brilliant. He spent a lot of time in Venice and I think that made me love it all the more. The art scene really dominated Venice, so if you are any kind of lover of art, Venice is the place to be. I did some of the canals, which were so romantic and relaxing. It really was a place I fell in love with and could spend more time in. Venice is also a city which is incorporated via a feeder route into the Via Francigena, the pilgrim route running through France to Rome.

MILAN

I also spent time in Milan, a beautifully organised city in the north. It is just an amazing city, and the new, architecturally stunning buildings sitting among ancient Roman ruins was just a feast for the eyes.

I caught up with my friends Lorenza and Italo. They lived outside the city in a more rural setting between Milan and Lake Como, with a beautiful dog called Ginni and some donkeys, bred by the owner of the farm and kept in a large pen at the back of the property. I saw a few gorgeous little ones. They had tufts of grey coat and were just so sweet. I helped Italo feed a few.

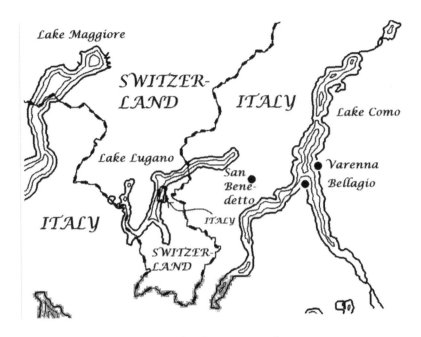

The Region of Lake Como and Varenna

There is still a great divide in Italy between the North and South. The North is more prosperous and industrial than the South, and all kinds of sociological reasons have been thought up to explain this. However, perhaps the simplest explanation is that the North is closer to the heart of Europe and its trade routes and markets—advantages long enjoyed by cities like Venice and Trieste—whereas the South is quite literally out on a limb. With improved roads and railways through the Alps in the nineteenth century, the gap only widened and it was no wonder that the major industrial cities of Italy then became Milan and Turin, in the north.

Meeting all the local farmers was interesting. Some of them supported the semi-separatist Northern League and some ran vineyards. All were hard workers. Even so, the number of unemployed men was quite high in the area in 2013.

I remember experiencing first hand why the Italian men are so famous for calling all the women 'Bella' ('beautiful' in English). One who was married asked me quite matter-of-factly if I'd like to get romantically involved with him. I was amazed he just made it all seem so normal and uncomplicated (it wouldn't have been!). I said no thanks and that was that.

I spent some of my time around Milan visiting the tourist destinations. Leonardo da Vinci's work is featured in and around many of the museums and galleries in Milan and that was reason enough to spend time looking at the more touristy places that I would usually avoid. I visited the Duomo di Milano, a magnificent cathedral from the fourteenth century and another

Milan Duomo (Cathedral) from the Southwest.
Photography by Steffen Schmitz ('Carschten'), June 2016,
Wikimedia Commons, CC-BY-SA 4.0.

place that pilgrims visited. The Duomo di Milano sits perfectly in the city centre with all the streets fanning out around it. I remember when I first laid eyes on it and I decided right there and then, before I even entered it, that it was one of my favourite churches that I had seen! It is just incredible.

I remember thinking, oh my, how did they build this in the fourteenth century? I later found out it wasn't actually completed until 1965. But still, the exterior and interior of the cathedral are impressive. Its highest point is over 100 metres high and it can hold about forty thousand people at a time, whch sounds extraordinary, but is true. It was originally begun by the Archbishop Antonio da Saluzzo as a reward for the working class and nobles of Milan who had suffered under a previous ruler.

Italian and Roman history just fascinate me, and I was making more connections with the Camino de Europa. I mean, really, you can't do a pilgrimage and not do Italy.

I really liked the part of Italy that Lorenza and Italo lived in - it had its own distinct character, quite different to the rest of the country.

When I visited Italo and Lorenza again in 2009, the economic collapse had become very prominent, and many Italian industries were closing down and Chinese ones opening up. The locals were getting really, really annoyed. Also, the bribery under Berlusconi had gone beyond any bounds. People who wanted to represent Italy in the Olympics had to bribe the mafia. I went to a party of women lawyers in Milan who were Lorenza's friends. Everyone smoked and drank wine throughout the meal, but I didn't, which was fine. When the conversation turned to healthy living and the consequences of excessive smoking and drinking, someone said, 'Why live?' And I thought, 'Well, that's interesting.' We never really drank wine in our household in Hastings — though we drank beer — and I did not grow up a smoker either, thank goodness in hindsight.

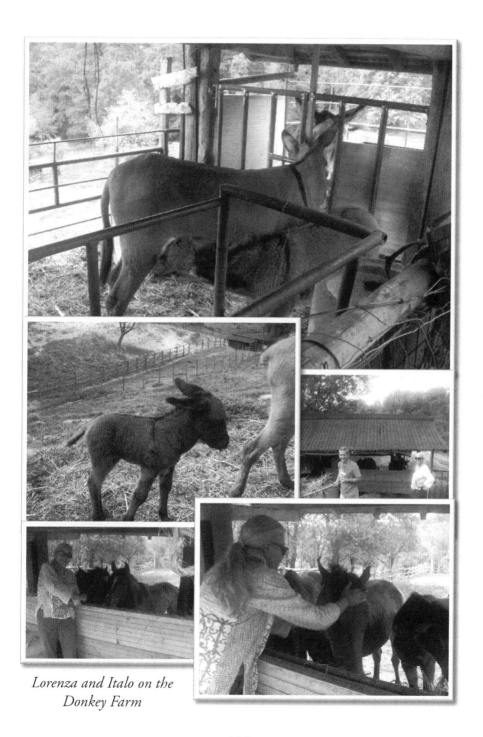

Lorenza and Italo on the
Donkey Farm

Lorenza's niece, Susanna, was there on this occasion: a successful business woman living in Barcelona. I also met one of Susanna's friends of Italian ancestry who was living in New York after marrying an American doctor. She was hoping to raise her children in Milan and had just convinced her husband to apply for a role in surgery there. He applied and somehow the mafia had intercepted his application and said they didn't want him to apply for a job in Milan. So, he turned to his wife and said that he was not going to live in Italy, that it was too corrupt and he didn't want to bring his children up in that society – which completely blew me away! I guessed there was probably more to that story than they let on or told me. I thought most people would want to live in Italy – I had sure found it tempting, especially in the more rural areas where it was all vineyards and rugged mountain ranges – and donkey farms!

I had earlier made a brief visit to Milan, and back then it seemed to be just a dirty town full of riff-raff. Visiting a second time and having the city reintroduced to me by Lorenza completely changed my views! Gone was the rubbish that used to litter the streets, replaced by beautifully paved and carefully arranged gardens. They had electric cars there which you could charge up and Lorenza had an apartment in the city which she rented out. The electric cars and other civic improvements reflected the competence of the local government, not Berlusconi's regime in Rome, as far as I could tell.

We went out for dinner often and one time we had pizza with tomato sauce and mozzarella and I became unwell. I said to Lorenza that I was gluten intolerant and she wanted to know why I didn't just ask for a gluten-free pizza. It was a fair point, although I hadn't even thought they would do gluten-free pizza. I also visited a very expensive chocolate shop in Milan and I bought 30 dollars' worth of a small amount of chocolates. I didn't think they were worth it, though.

We also went boating on Lake Como, from Varenna, and I've taken plenty of photos of that section of the trip!

On Lake Como

Varenna, on Lake Como

Varenna, Lake Como

Picturesque Varenna and its shaded alleys

Looking over Bellagio on Lake Como, to the mountain on which the eleventh-century Abbey of San Benedetto (St Benedict) stands. The whole Lake Como region, a sort of natural crossroads, is historically very important for pilgrims.

Perhaps my favourite picture of Lake Como

I did a number of trails around Milan which connect up with the Via Francigena. The full extended version of the Via Francigena runs all the way from Canterbury in England, then through Europe to Rome before a final stretch toward the Holy Land.

Turkey becomes part of this Camino and I visited parts of it when I went to Istanbul in 2000. The Via Francigena has its own version of the pilgrim's credencial that gets stamped at different points along the way. Many of these walks have only recently been recognised officially, well after I went there.

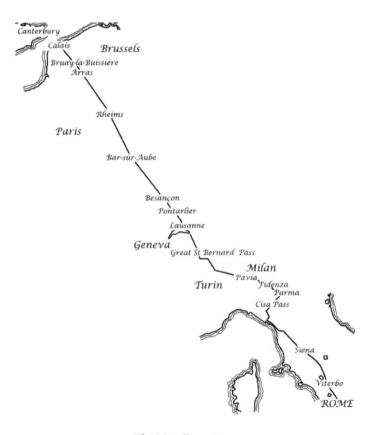

The Via Francigena
(Not to be confused with the French Way of the Camino de Santiago)

MONTE VISO

The Monte Viso is the highest peak in the Cottian Alps, which run along the border of France and Italy. I was trekking with my friend Jean-Claude. We weren't going to climb the peak but take a trek through the range. The official name of the trek we did was the 'Tour du Mont Viso'. The Cottian Alps have numerous treks and hikes throughout them, some following ancient Roman and French trade routes with historical sites along the way.

The Tour du Mont Viso actually crossed the border of France and Italy four times. I remember the boots I had brought with me to do the trek. I had brought them in Romania after sending my other ones back to New Zealand when I was in Switzerland on my way to Italy. I don't know what I was thinking. I think I got a bit desperate and brought a pair that was too small. Not a good thing to do on a long trek. After walking for five days, they were incredibly sore. I don't know how I continued on, but I did. Monte Viso was really beautiful. You can see Monte Viso from Mont Blanc, from the spires of Milan Cathedral, and even from the Klein Matterhorn in Switzerland. In Italy, Monte Viso is known as the Stone King, which I think is quite appropriate, too.

We stayed in a tent while we trekked and one night it got really cold, so Jean-Claude and I thought it'd be a good idea to put our sleeping bags together to keep warm. Well, Jean-Claude was not happy the next morning because he didn't get much sleep. I had tossed and turned and must have kept him up most of the night. I wasn't used to sharing my sleeping bag.

We ended up hiking as far up as 3,300 metres. There were many old hideouts built along the paths that were apparently from the time of Mussolini: military shelters that were part of the 1930s Vallo Alpino ('Alpine Wall') defensive line, I presume.

There are many legends surrounding Monte Viso. It is said that Hannibal built the tunnel 'Buco di Viso' below the Punta delle Traversette and used it to return to the north with his elephants. Actually, the tunnel was built in the 15th century for commercial reasons, mostly linked to salt trade.

One thing that is a fact is that near Monte Viso there is a Neolithic quarry for greenstone (jadeite), which the ancient inhabitants of Europe used to make 'cult axes' very similar to many Māori ceremonial artefacts, and which they transported all over Europe to give to one another in the same way that Māori transported greenstone and greenstone artefacts up and down the length of New Zealand from the remote mountain site where it is to be found in my country. You constantly find these parallels between cultures. But it is often a case of re-inventing the wheel, and some kind of far-fetched ancestral affinity should not be supposed without additional and less coincidence-like evidence to go on.

It was quite incredible to think about and actually see how interlinked Europe actually is. One minute we were in Italy and then the next we were in France.

My time in Italy had been a really good eye-opener and to actually see so much physical evidence of pilgrims in the medieval era made my pilgrimage all the more real. The Romans had achieved so much, creating some of the most important sites for religious people worldwide.

I have heard about a triangle-styled pilgrimage that goes from Rome, Tunisia and then to Jerusalem, and that got me quite interested too. I may explore that someday.

*A wayside map of the area we acclimatised in near Besmorello,
several ridges south of Monte Viso / A picturesquely isolated
house in our acclimatisation area*

*A picturesque structure
at San Bernolfo, another
mountain village in the area*

*Jean-Claude and
wayside signs in
the area where we
acclimatised to
climb Monte Viso*

*Further scenes from the
foothills near Monte Viso*

Shelters in the foothills, some intact, some ruined

Setting up Camp: What a View!

Climbing Monte Viso

It was nice to get back down, to somewhere more gentle

The Pyramid-like form of Monte Viso, also known as Monviso, dominates the surrounding ranges.

Source: Luca Bergamasco, Wikimedia Commons, 'Panoramica del gruppo del Monviso da Punta Ostanetta, con indicazione dei principali punti notevoli della cresta', CC-BY-3.0

255

CHAPTER ELEVEN
The English Are a Very Mixed Bunch

E NGLAND has many pilgrim trails, with more being developed of late. There is some kind of pilgrim revival going on due to its increasing popularity with the modern traveller.

Although I have no doubt that there were more original routes in England that lead to the St James's way, it is hard to find the original routes because of simple barriers like population growth and modern roads that have disrupted old pathways.

Also, thanks to Henry VIII, many of the sites and areas sacred to the Catholic people fell into ruin and were virtually forgotten about.

I have spent time working and living in England so it's familiar to me. I am no stranger to the English culture; I have travelled there many times and done a few walks since the 1980s. I really admire all the stunning churches around England.

Throughout the British Isles they have conjured up more and more information on pilgrim tours and trails, with many new places identified and new walks appearing.

The British Isles connection with the Iberian Peninsula and the St James's way goes back thousands of years and is deep-set in British blood. The DNA of the British Isles is something quite extraordinary, showing changes as people migrated, invaded and settled in the British Isles.

Going right back to the Bronze Age, DNA records show some of the earliest settlers were of Celtic and German descent from Central and Northern Europe. There have also been strong arguments for the presence of people from the Iberian Peninsula migrating and settling in Britain and Ireland.

Before and during Roman rule (43-410 CE), England was mostly inhabited by Britons, people speaking a language related to modern Cymraeg (Welsh).

After 410 CE, England occupied by Anglo-Saxons from Germany and their relatives the Danes. Germanic dialects replaced indigenous language in England. Britons in west who clung to old language dubbed Welsh, the Germanic word for Latin or Celt.*

Norman conquest (1066 CE) adds French overlay, thus creating modern English language in which simple or rude words are mostly Anglo-Saxon, lengthy or polite ones French or Latin.

Security from invasion, access to sea and abundant coal help to secure Industrial Revolution and global spread of the English language.

* The name of the Romanian province of Wallachia has the same origin.

Remains and ancient settlements are forever being discovered in this rich landscape, so whatever I mention here may very well change tomorrow. The earliest human settlement found in all the British Isles is an area in Devon that dates back more than forty thousand years. Since then, waves of migration have created distinct cultural influences throughout the British Isles.

Stonehenge is said to have been constructed well before the Bronze Age, in 3,100 BC, hinting at a thriving culture well before those introduced in the Bronze Age. Contemplating Stonehenge is quite tricky because there are many theories about who built it and why. One popular belief is that it was erected by Druids. The Druids bring to mind spiritual, wizardy, old guys worthy of appearing in *Lord-of-the-Rings*-type movies. Actually, the Druids

Roman Britain about 410 CE. Source: PCL.

began as a name for a group of highly educated people, usually men, and in occupations similar to what we know today as doctors and teachers. There was an element of religion to this group and that probably developed into something more spiritual, becoming the source of our *Lord-of-the-Rings-wizard-men* fantasy.

Three ancient tribal groups have been named and assumed to have been part of the groups who helped build Stonehenge, with or without the Druids. If this is true then they would share some similar cultural traits that motivated them to complete Stonehenge over different periods of time.

The earliest settlements within the Bronze Age identified one prominent cultural group called the Bell-Beaker Culture, described in older books as the Beaker Folk, who as the name suggests had worked out how to make earthenware drinking vessels ('beakers') that also flared out at the top, a bit like a bell. During the 12th century BCE there then seems to have been a change in cultural practices, which would point to a large-scale invasion, probably from Europe. The end of the Bronze Age and the beginning of the Iron age, around 1,200 BCE, was a time of great upheaval, as warriors with iron weapons attacked and defeated those who only had bronze ones, and many cultures changed at around this time.

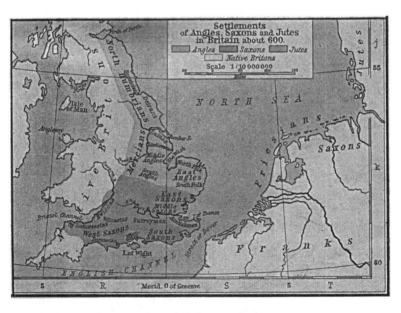

The Settlement of England circa 600 CE. Source: PCL.

It was during the Iron Age that there seemed to be a more overtly and obviously Celtic cultural influence. It was only later during the Iron Age that Germanic- and Celtic-speaking groups began to settle in the British Isles. The result was a more sophisticated culture that began using money and more developed technology in terms of jewellery, war craft, farming and transport. Prior to its conquest by the Romans, Britain was also the destination of many refugees from the Roman Empire-dominated Europe, so this added to the multi-cultural state of the British Isles.

From 122 CE, the Roman Empire held everything south of Hadrian's Wall, relaying a very obvious cultural influence throughout the British Isles. A stronger Anglo-Saxon presence in Britain is dated to somewhere in the fifth century, creating a Germanic cultural influence. It is thought that there was already Germanic influences and language within Britain even then, so it was more of a process over time.

Some of the first ancient pathways date back to the time of Stonehenge. Many of the routes and trails began as traders' routes across the channel between Britain and Europe as well as between neighbouring Scotland, Ireland and Wales. The walks throughout England evolved over time to include several pathways that were classed as one. For example, the route one might take in summer would differ from the one in winter due to environmental factors like flooding, and political ones like war. The routes would have been chosen for their convenience and accessibility to food, accommodation and water. Pilgrimages were popular in Europe well before they became popular in Britain.

Crossing the body of water that lay between Britain and Europe was a defining factor of British medieval pilgrims. When water travel wasn't an option, they resorted to pilgrimages within and around Britain. When St Augustine from Rome arrived in 595 CE, and then later died in Canterbury,

London: Hay's Galleria and 'the Shard'

this created one of the first pilgrimage sites in the British Isles. This was followed shortly after by St Thomas Becket, whose tomb is in Canterbury as well, and became another reason to visit this medieval place of pilgrimage. The numbers weren't large, but as Britain became more involved in the Catholic religion, the number of British saints grew, and therefore so did the

London: Top left, myself with a statue of Yoda. Top right, a Trooper of the Blues and Royals Regiment. Bottom, the Thames with Tower Bridge and the WWII light cruiser HMS Belfast

Fountain and Nelson's Column, Trafalgar Square

pilgrim sites for those seeking them. There are a few Pilgrim Way starting points in Britain from Canterbury, Bristol, Oxford, Plymouth, South Hampton and even Brighton that eventually find themselves joining the Camino de Santiago.

I have spent time in and around these areas. It is impossible to walk them as they originally were due to the loss of routes, as I mentioned before. When I was living in England, and on my many trips to England, I have done partial trails through Cumbria, including the Lake District and Somerset.

As I previously mentioned, Britain has renewed energy in developing pilgrim pathways around Britain and re-establishing old routes and trails. The Confraternity of St James is an organisation based in the United Kingdom that is dedicated to reconnecting the pathways through the British Isles back to Santiago.[1] There are trails with links to St James and churches to visit that are dedicated to him. One of these churches is located in Biddenham, which is from the 13th century and was built by the Normans.

The stained-glass windows, which date from Victorian and more recent times, are adorned with the scallop shell symbols.

There is another church in Croxton that has stained glass windows showing James, a staff and the scallop shells. There are more links around Britain through churches that add England securely into the Camino de Europa walks.

(It's worth noting that much of Britain's actual mediaeval heritage was destroyed in an ISIS-like fashion during later Protestant pogroms, because of its association with Roman Catholicism. Then, in the Victorian era, there was a great craze to try and revive such things as the art of making stained glass windows and gothic cathedrals. One consequence of this is that a lot

---

[1] The Confraternity of St James. (n.d.) Retrieved from http://www.csj.org.uk

of stuff that looks mediaeval in the old country is in reality no older than the Victorian-era gothic stonework in Christchurch, New Zealand – and just as *faux*. It is somebody's idea of the way things used to look in the old days, that is all. If the figures in the stained-glass windows, as at Biddenham, look photo-realistic, that is a dead giveaway that they are probably Victorian artwork and not genuine mediaeval artefacts, in which the people for the most part were clumsily drawn.)

In Britain, there is a national St James Day, one of the earliest occurring in 1314 held in the town of Blunham. In fact, there were several celebrations such as fairs and markets that were held in medieval times to celebrate St James.

These routes were part of the aforementioned Via Francigena, which begins in Canterbury, travels through Europe to Rome and then finally brings the pilgrim to Jerusalem in the Holy Land.

St Augustine landed in Canterbury to negotiate England's rule under the Pope, and it was the biggest success of his travels there. It was his mission from the Pope to convert the pagans to Christianity and the start of the Roman Catholic Church in England. Christianity had first arrived in Great Britain when the Romans occupied parts of England, and then spread to Ireland, Wales and Scotland. The last time that the Catholic Church in England was all-powerful was during the reign of Queen Mary (not to be confused with Mary Queen of Scots), in the 1550s.

Mary's successor Queen Elizabeth I, Mary's rival and half-sister, greatly weakened the Catholic Church's power, as she was a Protestant: a biological daughter of Henry VIII and ideologically his true successor, for it was of course Henry VIII who had first broken with Rome, a relationship briefly restored by Mary.

It was the Elizabethan Settlement by Queen Elizabeth I that removed the Church of England from under Rome's rule and made it an independent church – a reformed Protestant church. On top of that, the Methodist Church of England established itself away from the Church of England around the eighteenth century. It is known as a non-conformist church because it doesn't follow the rules of the Church of England, the official church, headed by the monarch.

There are pilgrim trails in England which are supported by the Protestant churches; a major new (old) one to be redeveloped is St Augustine's Way from Ramsgate to Canterbury, which connects up to the pilgrim ways in Europe.

CHAPTER TWELVE

Russia – A Very Underrated Part of Europe

Eastern Europe and Russia

> Kievan Rus founded 882. First united East Slavic state, based in Kiev. 'Rus' thought to refer to Vikings who helped found the kingdom.

> Mongol invasions contribute to fall of Kievan Rus in 1283

> Rise of Moscow. A duchy at first, but ruler Ivan IV ('the Terrible') styles himself Tsar, meaning Caesar or emperor, in 1547.

> Tsar Peter I ('the Great') founds new capital of St Petersburg and modernises Russia, early 1700s. Catherine the Great also significant.

> In the 1800s Russia lags behind the West. Russian Revolution 1917 sees Communist (Soviet Union) government, which in reality is brutally focused on modernisation and heavy industrial development. Soviet Union falls 1991.

ST PETERSBURG

I spent time in Russia in 2013. Russia would be one of the farthest reaches in Europe for pilgrims to journey. Russia has a beautiful history; lavish and almost luxurious, with well-presented historical places of real value on my pilgrim journey.

I suppose the pilgrim journeys began with the Kievan Rus, who were considered the ancestors of the people of Russia. The Kievan Rus were a group of loosely connected tribes in Eastern Europe around the 9th to 13th centuries. They created many routes around Russia by means of trade and pilgrimage – some of which are still there today.

I flew into St Petersburg and stayed in a hotel that I had booked online at booking dot com. I didn't hire a car, as I wasn't that confident in driving there. The hotel I had booked was extraordinarily expensive, about $220 a night, which was a lot of money for a pilgrim traveller. But I thought, well, why not? I suppose a few nights in a decent bed was well earned. I had a double bed and a balcony that opened up onto the river below. So, anyway,

I needed to use the internet. I am a landlord in New Zealand and I was looking after my rental properties. I still have to work when I travel – I have to check rent books, check my emails and keep in touch with my property manager and check in with what he is doing.

I went down to reception and they gave me the passwords. I remember the porter was standing there listening too. I logged onto the computer and looked at the Wi-Fi settings and saw 'Putin's network', which I thought was quite funny. Anyway, I decided that a double bed and a balcony with a view were not worth $220 a night, so I thought, blow it, and I looked for somewhere else to stay instead. I have a bit more to say about all this surveillance in *A Maverick Traveller*; I knew quite a few people in Greenpeace and I wonder in hindsight if I was mistaken for an activist, at a time when Greenpeace were occupying a Russian oil rig in the Arctic.

I ended up staying in a one-bedroom place with ten beds all in the one room. Most of the people who were staying there in that one room were Albanians. I ended up staying there for about four nights. It was a great location – easy to walk into town and easy to get on the tour buses. The tours from town were a lot cheaper too – about $100 a tour. I decided that as I was only here for five days, I would do five different tours.

One of the tours was to the Winter Palace. The Winter Palace is a grand building that was occupied by Peter the Great and his royal family in the 17th century. The exterior is richly decorated and when Catherine the Great came to the throne, she made further changes to the building, most unaltered to this day. I only walked around the outside of it because it was only open to the public on certain days. I remember the sky was like concrete; overcast and grey, but what a beautiful city.

St Petersburg: Winter Palace and Palace Square, birds-eye view with the General Staff Building at top. The Alexander Column can be seen in the middle of Palace Square, a square which is actually stirrup-shaped.

Photograph dated 14 July 2016. Source: Andrew Shiva / Wikimedia Commons / CC-BY-SA 4.0.

Standing in the archway in the middle of the General Staff Building façade on Palace Square (the Triumphal Arch of the General Staff), with the Alexander Column and Winter Palace in the background, during my recent trip to Russia

Palace Square, the Alexander Column, the Winter Palace by
night and the General Staff Building by day

273

Mariinsky Theatre

Peterhof Palace

Peterhof Palace

Peterhof is on the Shore

Equestrian statue (1782) of Peter the Great, dubbed 'The Bronze Horseman' by Pushkin. It stands on a plinth made from a 1500 tonne block of Finnish granite, transported part of the way by barge and part of the way by rolling it on a carpet of metal balls, one of the earliest known uses of ball bearings.

Catherine Palace at Tsarskoe Selo, on the outskirts of St Petersburg

Images of the destruction of the Catherine Palace in World War II,
taken from photographs hanging on the wall

Catherine Palace and Grounds (Catherine Parks), Tsarskoe Selo

Bathhouse Pavilion (top) and Grotto in Catherine Park, Tsarskoe Selo

*Church of the Saviour on Spilled Blood, erected on the spot
where Tsar Alexander II was assassinated in St Petersburg*

Mariinsky Palace and Theatre

I also did a beautiful night tour around the city of St Petersburg by bus. I loved seeing the city at night, which was totally different from seeing it by day. The grand palaces were all lit up and the beauty of it all was just breath-taking.

Every time I saw a Russian palace, I was gobsmacked. They really were as amazing as I had thought they would be, and splendid examples of Russian royal history. One tour was to the Mariinsky Palace, also known as the Marie Palace. It was the last Neoclassical palace to be built in St Petersburg and was built in the mid-19th century. Emperor Nicholas I gave the palace as a wedding gift to his daughter, Grand Duchess Maria Nikolaevna.

One thing I could not get over while I was in St Petersburg was the quality of the food. It was amazing. Everything was so fresh. I honestly believe that St Petersburg has the best restaurants in the world. You could order anything at all and the freshness was like everything had been picked straight out of the garden right there and then. One thing I hadn't really eaten a lot of before was beetroot salad. I had it a few times in St Petersburg and their beetroot salad had me sold. I just can't emphasise the quality and freshness of the food enough. I would love to go back to St Petersburg just for the food. It was all a reasonable price and fairly cheap for what you were paying for.

I decided to attend a theatre performance while I was in St Petersburg and looked up some theatres there. I found the historic Mariinsky Theatre, so I got some cheap tickets in the stalls and off I went. I found that the Mariinsky Theatre was not as traditional as the Bolshoi in Moscow, but I enjoyed it so much more than the Bolshoi performances. The Mariinsky seemed to be a more innovative sort of theatre, with more exciting costumes and variety in its performances.

Walking around St Petersburg with a backpack was a little frowned upon. To be honest, I don't think they saw many backpackers or pilgrim travellers. The pilgrim trails aren't as popular as in other countries; it hasn't quite caught up there. Nevertheless, the trails and routes are there thanks to the saints and people who made the journeys to Rome, the Holy Land and Santiago.

Very early on into the adoption of Christianity during the latter part of the ninth century, people set out from Russia on pilgrimages; mostly to Jerusalem and Palestine. The Russian Orthodox Church was the main influence in religion all over Russia, thought to have been founded by the Apostle Andrew. St Andrew is said to have arrived in Kiev and proclaimed that Russia would become a great Christian community. He erected a cross there, which was replaced by the St Andrew's Cathedral. Back then Russia encompassed Ukraine and Belarus, which brought it closer to its European Christian neighbours who helped bring Christianity to Russia. During the Kievan period, the Russian Orthodox Church was growing rapidly as the popular religion of the people. It was Byzantine Greek priests from Macedonia who translated the first Slavic-language Bible, meaning more people had access to the Christian texts. Without realising it, the Russians had paved the way to be indirectly influenced by Roman and Greek cultures.

The Greeks priests were involved in leadership of the churches founded in Russia, with the Greeks adding another country to their belt of countries successfully converted to the faith. Even with the Mongol, Polish and Swedish invasions of Russia, the churches still flourished and Russia saw a large increase in monasteries about the time of The Great Schism in 1054, which in essence was the division of the churches between East and West Europe. This saw the creation of the Russian Orthodox Church as it broke away from the Roman Catholic Church and became the 'Eastern' Church.

By the way, everyone uses the word Catholic but hardly anyone knows that it means. It means 'Diverse', 'Universal' or 'For Everyone'. If we say that someone has catholic tastes – with a small c, referring to matters mundane – that means they will try anything at a buffet: that they won't refuse anything foreign and exotic no matter how spicy. Anyhow, it goes without saying that all these schisms and separations gradually undermined the Catholic church's claim to universality and being for everyone, which also implies being suitable for everyone.

One thing that the Russian Orthodoxy was characterised by was its pilgrimages. They encouraged the worshipping of idols and icons, particularly when related to miracles.

The Russian Orthodox Church rates Jerusalem in the Holy Lands as an important place in their religion. Beyond religion, the Holy Land has high value for its role in the development of cultural, intellectual and political history of Russia. From very early in the adoption of Christianity within Russia and Eastern Europe, there are records of some of the first pilgrimages to Jerusalem down through Turkey. I think they would have had to be very committed to their religion – making such a long journey through harsh conditions and environments would not have always been the safest thing to do then.

Russian pilgrimages to Jerusalem were common right up until the nineteenth century. These later Russian pilgrims left us some valuable information about their journeys, the routes, the dangers and their first impressions of the Holy Lands. There is a valuable piece of historical evidence found in a book from the early nineteenth century (so it's not super ancient, or anything) of written accounts of their pilgrimages called the *Way of a Pilgrim*.[1]

Russia adopted the Orthodox Church rules into their government system during the Romanov dynasty. They incorporated much of the Greek Orthodox Church's ideologies and pursued to align their policies and ideas more closely with that of Greece. Eastern Orthodoxy, as it is often

---

[1] Hermitary (2006). The way of a pilgrim: A Russian Orthodox hermit's path. Retrieved from http://www.hermitary.com/articles/pilgrim.html

called, is organised in such a way that each country has its own Orthodox church: Greek Orthodox, Russian Orthodox, Bulgarian Orthodox, Serbian Orthodox, and so on. But they are all fundamentally the same thing, and the different names reflect the fact of national organisation.

It was during the 19th century that Russia established a solid presence in the Holy Land, teaching other Orthodox peoples – a minority in the mostly Islamic territories – in the academics and intellectual subjects of the Orthodox religion. Eventually a Palestinian Orthodox society was established based on the Russian Orthodoxy's teachings and ideas – I thought this was quite amazing! The Russian Orthodox faith even incorporated its ideas in architecture and the decoration of buildings around Moscow and St Petersburg and I got to see a lot of this in the palaces and museums I visited – it's still all there today.

One of the more important pilgrim sites is in Kiev, in Ukraine, which is considered the birthplace of Russia via Kievan Rus. It is the Monastery of the Caves (Pechersk Lavra), which are said to have been created by two Russian saints, St Anthony and St Theodosius.

Again, another theme of my travels was apparent here in Russia: war and invasion disrupted and divided some of the major Christian religions. Some of the churches were seized by Catharine the Great's predecessor, Peter III (her husband, who was assassinated). Catherine continued seizing the church estates for the crown, though in later years she changed her mind and allowed more religious freedom.

I did a tour around Pushkin, 30 km south of St Petersburg, where Catherine the Great's and Peter the Great's palaces are located. Catherine was known for her extravagance and ordered a German architect to build her a summer palace in 1717 for no other reason than for her pleasure. More than 100 kg of gold was used to decorate the exterior facades of the

325-metre-long palace. The Peterhof Palace, based on one of the homes of Peter the Great, is known as the Russian Versailles for its position looking out over the Gulf of Finland. The gardens with their many fountains are a central feature of this palace built in the 18th century. I remember looking out over the water to Finland and thinking that I was going to go there one day.

While I was on these tours, I met two people. One was a guy named George who was looking for a Russian wife, and the other one was an older guy who was a retired scientist. We all had plenty of interesting discussions and I learnt more about Russian history. One thing I learnt about was the Crimean Peninsula, home to plenty of Greek ruin. Crimea was once a colony of ancient Greece. It remained that way for some time and has a long history behind it. The name the Greeks gave the area was Taurica. Crimea, like the Iberian Peninsula, had been the source of conflict between many countries trying to claim it, most recently between Russia and Ukraine in 2014.

The most notable war, the Crimean War was fought between France, the Ottoman Empire, the British Empire and Sardinia on one side, and Russia on the other, from 1853 to 1856. The inclusion of Sardinia is not a misprint; as incredible as it sounds, the Kingdom of Sardinia was one of Europe's great powers at this time, mainly because it included a sizeable chunk of northern mainland Italy as well. Its red, white and green flag would become the flag of Italy when Italy was eventually unified.

The Crimean War finally ended with the Treaty of Paris, basically a draw in which Crimea was restored to the Russian Empire and both Russia and Turkey were barred from establishing bases on the Black Sea coast at locations that might threaten each other. The present troubles in and around Crimea have little to do with the Crimean War, and stem from the

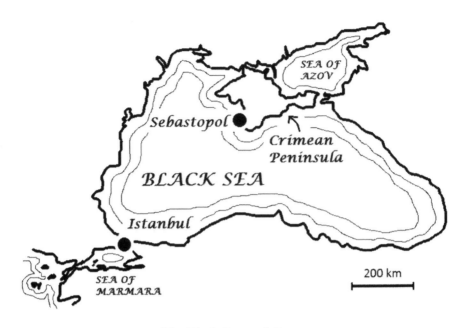

The Black Sea and Crimea

fact that Crimea was assigned from Russia to the Ukraine in 1954 by the Soviet leadership, at a time when this was an administrative decision of little consequence since the Soviet Union was all-powerful and countries within it, such as Russia and the Ukraine, merely ciphers. It lit a fuse that would only start to burn in earnest when, suddenly, the Soviet Union disappeared.

Crimea is home to the oldest church in Eastern Europe, the Church of St John the Baptist built in 717 CE, making it a very important place to visit as part of a pilgrimage around Russia. Apparently, there are a few historical sites that were also moved to Moscow during the world wars to protect them from being destroyed.

I mingled more with the locals when I was staying in St Petersburg. There were many Albanian girls who were working in the kitchen at the hostel I was staying in. I remember them telling me that they were only paid about $50 a week and that that's what most girls who go to work in St Petersburg were getting. I thought, my goodness, that is a low wage to be getting! I did learn, though, while talking more with the girls, that most people in careers like cleaning and receptionists only earn about $160 a month! Although my trip was a little up and down at times, I would really like to go back again. I think I would like to try skiing near St Petersburg.

MOSCOW

I had intended to go to Belarus next after St Petersburg. I had heard that the drinking water there was something I had to be careful of because it was close to Chernobyl. I headed to the Belarus Embassy in St Petersburg where I was applying for my visa. I was travelling on my British passport and had put my initial application in under my British passport. I think if I had used my New Zealand passport, I would have got through to Belarus without a problem, but they seemed to be delaying my application. I wasn't organised enough and decided in the end I'd just forget about it and go to Moscow instead.

I ended up getting a train from St Petersburg to Moscow and my overall first impression was how dreary it was. The sky was overcast and grey. My actual train ride was interesting, and I did enjoy it. What I loved about the Russian trains was that they actually had places where you could hang up your coats, which I thought was most civilised. I could see how the Russians do have a cultural pride. Russian culture grew from that of the East Slavs with their pagan beliefs and specific way of life in the wooded areas of Eastern Europe and then became urban, with Greek and then French and German influences.

The Metro Stations there in Russia were fantastic, I thought. They were beautiful buildings, mostly built before, during and after World War II. Mostly unchanged since then, they were however in bad repair and they became susceptible to power cuts and people would get trapped there. Luckily, I never got trapped when I was there, thankfully.

I arrived in Moscow and had planned to stay for a short while at a youth hostel that I found was run by an American. I was amazed at the number of Americans living in Moscow. They were running hostels or working as teachers, although they didn't get well paid as teachers there.

I did a lot of walking around Moscow. I visited Red Square, which is the intersection of Moscow's main streets. The square, or plaza, is site to the official residence of the president and was the site of many historic ceremonies, proclamations and events. The square has been around since the early 15thcentury and is surrounded by churches. When I went there the Red Square was cordoned off, though I don't know why. So, instead I wandered around. I remember I took a lot of photos and I went to a number of Russian Orthodox Churches from the 15th century. I thought that a lot of churches were destroyed in 1917 with the Bolshevik Revolution. To my surprise, there were still a lot of churches and cathedrals around the Red Square. I visited three cathedrals around Moscow's Red Square, including the St Basil's Cathedral, the Cathedral of the Archangel and the Kazan Cathedral. All three were really stunning and they had a lot of 15th century art work which I was really impressed with.

I visited the fortified part of the city known as Moscow Kremlin, which is the official residence of the President of Russia. The name Kremlin literally translates to citadel. It was really nice and not far from the Red Square, overlooking the Moskva River. It was built in the 14th century and is listed as a UNESCO World Heritage Site.

The Moscow Kremlin (i.e., 'Citadel'), birds-eye view. This interesting image, first published in 2008, shows the Grand Kremlin Palace in the centre foreground to be part-way through a process of being restored from what appears to be bare red brick as per the Kremlin walls and towers, to a peach plaster surface. The Moscow River is at bottom right. Source: www.kremlin.ru, CC- BY-4.0.

The Kremlin Walls, from the Moscow River Embankment (taken on my recent trip).

The Grand Kremlin Palace as I saw it recently, from outside and inside the walls

Grand Kremlin Palace, colonnade, also visible in birds-eye view

Cathedral of the Annunciation, behind Kremlin Wall

*In the grounds of the Kremlin with the
Kremlin Cathedrals, the Tsar Cannon
(each ball weighs a tonne) and the
view from a palace window*

Cathedral of the Annunciation

Cathedral of the Twelve Apostles, next to the Cathedral of the Dormition

Cathedral of the Dormition

(Dormition is an Orthodox term with a similar meaning to Assumption in Roman Catholicism, so this building is also known in English as the Cathedral of the Assumption)

*Closer views of exterior frescoes on Kremlin Cathedrals,
in varying states of restoration.*

The Kremlin Arsenal. The cannons were captured from Napoleon during his ill-fated invasion of Russia.

The Troitskaya and Spasskaya Gate towers of the Kremlin, at top. Below, the Iberian Gate of the old city of Kitay-Gorod and the Little Chapel.

Kazan Cathedral (top) and the Cathedral of Christ the Saviour

By the eternal flame in the Alexander Gardens near Red Square

The Four Seasons statue in Manezhnaya Square, by the Alexander Gardens

*Italian grotto in the Alexander Gardens; parklands; monument
to the assassinated Tsaw ('Imperator') Alexander II near the
Cathedral of Christ the Saviour*

The Bolshoi Theatre

*St Basil's Cathedral with 1818 monument to
Russian national heroes Minin and Pozharsky*

St Basil's Cathedral

Inside St Basil's

St Basil's Interior, further details

*More gorgeousness
from inside St Basil's*

Pushkin Museum of Fine Arts, top; Tretyakov Gallery, below.

*Modern Sculptures, from the
serious to the humorous*

Zorab Tsereteli's controversial, kitschy, 86-metre statue of Peter the Great

Collages on display in a Moscow modern art museum

The Moscow Metro

*Stained Glass
Window in
Metro Station
(presumably
vandalism no
problem)*

Sometimes to get to know a city well you just need to walk around, getting lost and stumbling on places you might otherwise have missed,which is exactly what happened to me. I stumbled quite accidently onto the Museum of Modern Art. When I visited, they had an exhibition running with a temporary collection on display with a theme on democracy. It was unbelievable and amazing that such a place could exist in St Petersburg. So, you know what? Russians do get their say, and democracy does exist here. Now I really do object to the Western views of Russia that they are without democracy.

The Museum of Modern Art had amazing art work that had been donated by George Costakis. Born in 1913, his art collection became the biggest collection of modern Russian avant-garde art in the world. He had saved all this amazing art work by Russian artists, defying the Soviet politics at the time. I thought he was a pretty amazing guy. The world is a funny place; how sad that half of his artwork is in Greece, and then Greek artwork is throughout the Vatican in Italy.

I didn't realise it at the time, but I walked right through an area that had been the site of the Battle of Moscow in 1612. It was a war between Russian and Polish-Lithuanian forces. The Polish-Lithuanian forces were trying to break through to the Moscow Kremlin, besieging the city.

Russia has plenty of good pilgrim sites; it's just that people aren't always aware of them. All the information on the pilgrim trails comes from other countries, such as the St Olav's Way that goes from Russia into Norway. Only Norway has readily available information on it. Don't let that put you off, though. Russia is a rich nation in terms of pilgrim sites and walks.

CHAPTER THIRTEEN
Eastern Europe

> In Roman times, Slavs lived to northeast in modern Ukraine and neighbouring areas. The Magyar (Hungarians) lived in Siberia.

> Before 1000 CE, Slavs expand into modern Russia, central Europe and the Balkans. Romanians (speaking language descended from Latin) and Magyar occupy band between Balkan or South ('Yug') Slavs and other Slavs.

> Eastern Europe heavily affected by Mongol invasions, set back relative to West. Lack of seaports also hampers trade and development. Lag behind West becomes chronic in spite of efforts to catch up.

> Many Eastern European countries gain independence in late 1800s and early 1900s. Map of the region still changing in more recent times.

CROATIA

The thing about travel is you never know which cities you will love or dislike. One place I didn't think I'd enjoy was Croatia, but I loved it. I really, really did. I took the bus from Trieste in Italy to Croatia's capital city, Dubrovnik.

Roman Catholicism is the prevalent religion in Croatia – not surprising given it is right opposite Italy, sharing the same body of water. Croatia is a popular area of pilgrimage for Serbians, and because of Croatia's proximity to Italy, it has pilgrim sites along the length of the Croatian coastline. The latest figures show that there are fewer numbers for Muslims, Protestants and Eastern Orthodox.

Dubrovnik was beautiful. I loved how old the city was. It sits along the cliffs above the Adriatic Sea and is encircled by a historical wall that is still standing in most parts of the city. Parts of it are from as far back as the twelfth century. I think *mesmerising* is the right word to use when describing Croatia – it really was stunning. The entire city is listed as a UNESCO World Heritage Site. The main street in Dubrovnik makes you feel as though you've been transported back in time. Orange tiled roofs atop white-washed square buildings; it has such a raw, earthy beauty about it that I found completely captivating.

I stayed right in the city in a beautiful place with striking views. I also took a ferry around the national parks within Dubrovnik and got off on an

'Dubrovnik, Old Town with City Walls'.
Photograph by 'Bracodbk', Wikimedia Commons, 21 June 2011, CC-BY-SA 3.0.

island where I walked around for a few hours. The crew were all drinking beer behind the counter, I noticed this when I went to use the toilet. Dubrovnik itself, an ancient walled city, was beautiful and extraordinary, its Old Town a UNESCO World Heritage site.

The Way of Mary is the main pilgrim trail through Croatia, and follows the coastline before crossing into other countries like Bosnia-Herzegovina.

BOSNIA-HERZEGOVINA

I never intended to stop in Bosnia-Herzegovina, but just pass through it en route to Montenegro. I found Bosnia-Herzegovina to be quite an oppressive country. It was cold and I had not heard wonderful things about it. The devastating civil wars that had happened so recently left a bad taste in my mouth.

The bus route I took from Croatia took me along the coastline and over the border into the town of Medjugorje, a major Catholic pilgrim site. There is a St James Church here, reflecting again the importance the apostle had all over Europe, even as far east as Bosnia-Herzegovina. The Croatian Mary's Way passes through here on its way to Slovenia and Poland; it has its own marker used like the St James's way scallop shells. The Mary's Way uses the letter M with a cross in the middle.

Bosnia-Herzegovina amazed me with its different religions, split pretty much 50:50 with Christianity and Islam. The number of mosques around the city centre did amaze me. I only spent one night in Bosnia-Herzegovina and for me that was enough. I got back on the bus to Montenegro, another country jaded by civil wars and racial tensions.

Zagreb Main Railway Station, and the New Town of Belgrade by night from Kalemegdan Park in Old Belgrade, with the statue of the Victor (Pobednik), across the confluence of the Danube and Sava rivers.

SERBIA

I got to Belgrade in Serbia. One thing that stood out was the sweet corn. The Serbians loved the stuff and there was a vast range of food and drinks that were made from sweet corn! I found the food was not to my liking; my gluten intolerance did not go down well with the Serbians' love of pastries.

Serbia was an important place for me to visit on my travels through Europe along the ancient lines of the Camino de Europa. Serbia was once inhabited by Celtic tribes and afterwards was part of the Roman Empire, followed by the Christianisation of Serbia by the Byzantines in the ninth century. The very first Christian Roman Emperor was born with the boundaries of modern-day Serbia. For these reasons alone Serbia was an important pilgrim stop for me on my journey.

The Serbian language is part of the Slavic group of languages; it is more formally known as Serbo-Croatian, a mixture of the two dialects and used widely through Eastern and Western Europe. It is recognised as the official language in Serbia and Bosnia-Herzegovina. It is one of the few languages that use Cyrillic and Roman alphabets simultaneously.

The Cathedral of St Sava is the second largest Eastern Orthodox church in the world, and a fascinating building. The church is dedicated to St Sava, a prominent medieval figure and a martyr for the revolt against the Ottoman Empire. The cathedral was built over the ground where St Sava's remains were burned. It is a massive, grand, white building with deep blue and brown domes atop it. The construction began in the late 1800s, but the outbreak of wars in the Balkans, followed by World War One, meant it wasn't officially started until 1935 – 340 years after St Sava had died. In World War II, construction was halted again and the German Army used the area as a parking lot. Construction began again in 1985. So, it is by no

St Sava and St Marks, Belgrade.

Both images Wikimedia Commons. Upper photogaph by 'Skelenard', 12 November 2016, CC-BY-SA 4.0. Lower photograph by 'Litany', 18 May 2007, CC-BY-SA 3.0.

means ancient or old, and that's one theme I noticed when travelling this far east: plenty of historical sites that had been disrupted by war. It was quite sad.

The Eastern Orthodox Church in Serbia, the Serbian Orthodox Church, is the second-oldest branch of Eastern Orthodoxy in the world, and is the major religion there. It is also the main religion in Bosnia-Herzegovina. Christianity spread to the area historically known as the Balkans (in Southeastern Europe), as early as the first century, following the invasion of Slavic groups into the area. Christianity became a popular religion in modern-day Serbia in the six and seventh centuries.

The Great Migrations of the Serbs were another historically significant religious movement. Thousands of Serbs had to flee Serbia and headed in the direction of the Habsburg Empire to escape the control of the Ottoman Empire. The first migration occurred in 1690 during the Austro-Turkish War of 1683–1699, when a revolt against Ottoman rule failed. Fearing reprisals, tens of thousands of Serbs migrated into Habsburg territory. The Habsburg Empire was an Austrian empire that was part of the Holy Roman Empire and ruled territories under its jurisdiction. Most of the Serb people settled in what is now Hungary. Eventually, the Kingdom of Serbia became part of the Habsburg Empire, until another uprising by the Ottoman Empire that led to the return of the land to the Islamic faith, sparking a second migration of Christian Serbs from 1739.

Serbia is also tied in sadly with Medjugorje, the Catholic pilgrim site in Bosnia-Herzegovina. Eight hundred Orthodox Christian Serbians were massacred here by the Croatian Catholic Nazis. The story is quite haunting. Medjugorje has now become one of the most popular Catholic pilgrim sites in the world following apparitions of the Blessed Virgin Mary to six local children in 1981.

The routes of these historic trails and tragedies have formed some of the pilgrim trails in and around Serbia. I've heard that Russia and Serbia are working together to connect the trails of pilgrim sites between the two countries and are going to create an official pilgrim trail. I am quite excited to see what becomes of this.

BULGARIA

Bulgaria is a large country that sits directly to the north of European Turkey. The main religion is Bulgarian Orthodox, but there are also Catholics and Jewish people here. What surprised me most was that around 12% of the population is Muslim, with a very large Turkish minority. I stayed in Sofia, the capital of Bulgaria, and I noticed there were a lot of Greek influences in the buildings and architecture.

I saw a few of the Orthodox churches there and it really hit home to me how interested I was in the Orthodox faith. I always make a point of visiting churches and religious houses, but I feel slightly more drawn to the Orthodox churches. I went to Sofia's very well-known square of religious tolerance where the Banya Bashi Mosque (Islam), St Nedelya Church (Orthodox), St Joseph's Cathedral (Catholic) and the Sofia Synagogue (Jewish) all sit side by side. I thought it was interesting that Bulgaria had such a public acknowledgement of these four different religions looking out onto one another. It just shows how far some countries have come. Christianity was established in the boundaries of what is modern-day Bulgaria around the ninth century, a similar time to neighbouring countries.

It was time to move on to other parts of Eastern Europe and learn some more!

Bulgaria

All images Wikimedia Commons. Top image St. Alexander Nevsky Cathedral,
Sofia, © Plamen Agov • studiolemontree.com 'MrPanyGoff', 5 November 2010,
CC-BY-SA 4.0. Bottom left image Plovdiv Regional Ethnographic Museum, by
Dennis Jarvis, 6 May 2012, CC-BY-SA 2.0. Bottom right image Street in Old
Town, Plovdiv, by Jeroen Kransen, 18 May 2006, CC-BY-SA 2.5.

ROMANIA

Romania is another mostly Eastern Orthodox country, with the other main religions there being Roman Catholicism and Protestantism. It is a secular state with no single religion claimed by the country.

One thing I did learn plenty about during my travels is the variety of different denominations within each religion; the Eastern Orthodox religion is then divided again by which country it is practised in, and the same with Catholicism.

I went to Bucharest, the capital city, which was a very modern city. The city was actually quite stunning with amazing architecture and extremely exuberant palaces. It was not the dodgy, underdeveloped, war-torn country I thought it would be. I stayed in a hostel run by a Jewish family. I was fascinated by the Romanian Orthodox religion and I visited a few of their churches while I was there. The modern-day Romanian Orthodox Church is only second in size to the Russian Orthodoxy. I also found that in Bucharest there was a strong Catholic presence with many cathedrals in the city.

I found it very easy to find my way around because the Romanian language is actually similar to French and Spanish, as it is actually an Eastern Romance language.

I visited the Romanian Orthodox Patriarchal Church[1] that was built in the 1600s and has survived wars and devastating dictatorship. The paintings on the inner walls are such a delicate detail of the church. It is the destination of pilgrimages made on Palm Sunday around Bucharest.

[1] Popescu, I (2015, Dec 28). Religious Romania: Churches and monasteries that attract the largest crowds of pilgrims every year. *Discover Romania*. Retrieved from http://www.romania-insider.com/religious-romania-churches-and-monasteries-that-attract-the-largest-crowds-of-pilgrims-every-year

HUNGARY

By the time I reached Hungary, I was pretty exhausted and I went up into the hills around Budapest to relax in the Turkish baths. It was a brilliant thing to relax in baths that were built during the Ottoman Empire – *real* Turkish baths in other words, not just a figure of speech – and as old as they were, I came out feeling fresh and clean. Budapest has plenty of natural thermal pools in and around the city and I've heard it called the 'city of baths'.

I was travelling with a friend and it was the first time either of us had ever tried goulash before. We were served it as one of our meals at a hostel. I hadn't tasted anything quite like it and wasn't entirely sure what to make of it.

Hungary is a treasure trove of beautiful buildings and places; a tourist's and pilgrim's dream. The city was such a mixture (as I have found many cities in Europe to be) of old and modern influences can be seen in the baths and the architecture throughout Budapest. As always, I began my exploration throughout the city's streets and popular 'Ways' to see all the local sites. One thing that struck me was how harmoniously everything seemed to blend together. Of course, there were a few moments where the splendour was dampened by memories of the wars, but overall it was a lovely place. Christianity is the dominant form of religion throughout the country: Catholics, Lutherans, and others make up the majority of faith held by Hungarians. Hungary has adopted Christianity as its main religion since 1000 CE, making it a significant influence in the country's growth and development. While I was in Hungary, though, I did notice that there seemed to be a lack of religious practice compared to other parts of Eastern Europe I had been to. The country seemed more secular and Westernised.

I suppose, though, most people don't go to Hungary for religion, they go for the baths!

Gellért Baths Budapest.

Images Wikimedia Commons. Top left photograph by József Rozsnyai, 1 July 2013, CC-BY-SA 3.0. Architecturally rectified and trimmed for this book. Top right image by Denis Barthel, 2004, CC-BY-SA 3.0. Bottom Image by Thaler Tamas, 9 January 2014, CC-BY-SA 3.0.

Gellért Baths, Budapest.
All images Wikimedia Commons by 'Christo', 24-26 September 2016, CC-BY-SA 4.0.

327

St Martin's pilgrim routes are very popular through Hungary and directly related to Santiago de Compostela. St Martin was Bishop of Tours which became a shrine and a major stop for pilgrims in France en-route to the cathedral in Spain. St Martin is also closely associated with Hungary, as it is the country of his birth. St Martin is known as the patron of beggars. One night he saw a beggar to whom he gave his cloak, and that beggar turned out to be Jesus. His empathy and kindness made him extremely popular with the general population of Christians. Hungary holds a St Martin's day every year, which is also called the Goose and Wine Festival. The St Martin of Tours cultural route is one that connects many European towns that are associated with the life of the saint, connecting Hungary to France and then on to Santiago.

The second major reason for pilgrimage in Hungary was to visit a relic has been held in the country for over 800 years: that of the English saint Thomas Becket. A fragment of bone that is said to have belonged to Thomas Becket has been housed in the Basilica of Esztergom in Hungary. Becket's popularity is not just with Catholics, but with people from the Anglican Church as well.

I can't say that I have walked these routes, yet! But it is something I am willing to try next time I visit. I did, however, get a chance to have a look at some of the churches within Budapest, and my friend and I did do a fair bit of exploring by foot. We saw the majestic Matthias Church as well as the St Stephen's Basilica.

The people there were pretty friendly, and I found many were not native Hungarians but from other neighbouring countries also. There were many tales of coming to Hungary for a better life, just as I'm sure there are many who left Hungary for a better life too.

POLAND

Poland was a country that surprised me. It doesn't seem to matter where I go, the pilgrim trails stretch as far and wide as possible.

The roots of Christianity in the area can be traced back as far as 966 CE, well before Poland was an established country. Gorka Klasztorna is the oldest shrine for pilgrims within Poland, and the country's religious sites not only attract millions of Catholic pilgrims, but Jewish pilgrims as well.

I spent most of my time in Warsaw, the capital city, and saw haunting memories of Poland's turbulent past alongside historical sites and buildings. In Warsaw, there is the famed Krakowskie Przedmieście street, part of the

Warsaw 1944 Uprising re-enactors outside the
Ministry of Culture and National Heritage

329

Royal Route past historical and religious sites within Warsaw's city centre. The trail runs a circuit through the main city based on a 15th century trading route – quite an education on Polish history, I found.

Poland is made up of a vast range of religious groups – mostly Catholic, but Orthodox Christians, Buddhists and Jews live here as well.

Warsaw: Ornate street lights, and the Presidential Palace

*Warsaw: St Anne's Church, dating back to 1788,
and Krakowski Przedmieśce on the Royal Route*

*Warsaw: the Visitationist Church (top) and the Potocki Palace,
headquarters of the Ministry of Culture and National Heritage*

Adam Mickiewicz Monument (above), Carmelite Church below

Warsaw: Public Demonstration, and overview

Warsaw

I loved the Late Baroque-style architecture (Rococo), of which the Carmelite Church was a prime example. The front façade was embellished with carvings and statues, with a dome sitting atop the centre. Construction was started on the church in 1692 and not completed until 1761, making it a historical treasure nestled in among Warsaw's busy streets.

I also saw the monument of revered Adam Mickiewicz, a talented poet, writer and political activist. He was involved with the Crimean War, helping direct Polish and Jewish forces alongside the British, French, Turks and Sardinians, against Russia. Mickiewicz died halfway through the war in Istanbul, or Constantinople as it then was. There is a museum dedicated to his memory in Istanbul, organised around the apartment in which he lived and his temporary gravesite beneath it. Mickiewicz's remains were transported to France soon after his death, and finally arrived in Kraków in 1890. As a Polish nationalist Mickiewicz's quarrel had mainly been with the Russians, who ruled most of the historical territory of Poland in those days. Kraków was in a small corner of Poland administered at that time by the Austrians. The Austrians encouraged Polish nationalism so long as it was mainly anti-Russian in form, and were happy to allow Mickiewicz to be buried on the bit of Polish soil that they controlled.

Poland is peppered with pilgrim sites and significant churches and such, but there is one site that is more prominent then the rest: The Shrine of Divine Mercy in Krakow. It was one of the places I desperately wanted to see, but sadly I found I just simply lacked the time. I did, however, get to see the St Stanislaus Kostka Church in Warsaw. It is dedicated to a modern martyr, a priest who was assassinated in the 1980s and beatified (a step on the way to sainthood) in 2010.It was made a popular pilgrim destination in Warsaw when Pope John Paul II visited his gravesite in 1987, and since had over 20 million pilgrims visit.

I discovered that there is a route from Poland to Santiago in Spain, the Lesser Polish Way of St James, accompanied by its own scallop shell insignias. This route runs from Sandomierz to Krakow through the Land of Lesser Poland, an area in the south of Poland. It then joins up with the Via Regia (an old Roman route) through Germany and then onwards to Spain. The trail was officially opened again to the public from start to finish in 2009, so is another more recent addition to the routes of the Camino de Europa.

The world's fascination with religion is quite amazing, and a brilliant, yet humble, adventure to be a part of.

Conclusion

Europe is so complex – interrelated, yet divided.

I love mixing with the locals. I probably missed many of the sites because of it but, I felt I have accomplished a lot. Climbing mountains and walking, to me, is much more fascinating than riding a Ferris wheel or dining out at fancy restaurants. Cheap street food is more my cup of tea and I found it tastier than the more expensive places. Markets were even better – fresh from the local farms and ready for sale.

Along my travels I found that Islam, Christians and Jews all come from the same background of religious rules. All their religious books have similar grounding and similar stories in them. It just shows how much we – they – all have in common. It seems to be the commonalities that divide us.

Whichever way my feet ended up taking me – north, south, east or west – I can look back now and see (and know) that I have racked up a fair bit of mileage on the Camino de Europa and I am lucky to have gone as far as I have. I imagine how difficult it would have been for pilgrims during the Middle Ages and the like.

Travelling doesn't always have to be about religion or be a spiritual journey, but it can be just for the pure enjoyment of learning about another culture, making friends and some of those friendships lasting a long time. I discovered plenty about religion and each country's tolerance and preferences; each church, mosque, temple, basilica and synagogue amazing me just as much as the last. It was even better to walk along the same ancient pathways and routes as so many before me had, with very little and in harsher conditions than myself.

I can't say I found an awe-inspiring reason for everyone to take up their walking boots and packs and start walking, but it was a journey of education just as much as it was a journey of learning about religion, which I suppose was a central reason for me heading off into the dusty horizon. It was a journey that I can now reflect on, and look back on with pride and humbleness at the same time. I am forever thankful for the opportunities and the ability to get among the everyday hustle and bustle of other people's lives. I have learnt a great deal.

Pilgrims of all religions have walked these trails and let us hope all the renewed interest in them can help, so all can enjoy them, no matter their religion or reasons.

APPENDIX
Useful Websites

CAMINO DE EUROPA

http://www.caminosantiagodecompostela.com
https://en.wikipedia.org/wiki/Via_Imperii
https://en.wikipedia.org/wiki/Via_Regia
https://en.wikipedia.org/wiki/List_of_Christian_pilgrimage_sites

CAMINO DE ST JAMES – SANTIAGO DE COMPOSTELA

http://www.caminosantiagodecompostela.com
http://santiago-compostela.net
http://caminoways.com

GREECE AND TURKEY

http://www.pilgrimroutes.com/greece.aspx
http://cultureroutesinturkey.com/st-paul-trail
http://www.goreme.com/derinkuyu-underground-city.php

IRELAND

http://www.pilgrimpath.ie
http://www.aranislands.ie/tochar-walking-ireland-s-ancient-pilgrim-paths
http://www.saintsandstones.net/stones-leabadhiarmada-journey.htm

SCOTLAND

http://www.scotlandspilgrimjourneys.com
http://www.walkhighlands.co.uk/west-highland-way.shtml

GERMANY

http://www.germany.travel/en/specials/spiritual-travel/traditions-and-customs/pilgrimage-routes/pilgrimage-routes.html
http://www.deutsche-jakobswege.de/wege-uebersicht.html

AUSTRIA

https://www.innsbruck.info/en/map/tours/tour/pilgrim-route-the-way-of-st-james-ellboegen-iglsvill.html
http://www.salzburgerland.com/en/spiritual/pilgrimage-routes.html

SAXON SWITZERLAND

http://www.csj.org.uk/planning-your-pilgrimage/routes-from-further-afield/swiss-route-jakobsweg

SPAIN

http://www.travelwithachallenge.com/Spanish_Walking_Tour.htm

FRANCE

http://walkinginfrance.info/appendices/traditional-french-pilgrim-routes
http://www.csj.org.uk/planning-your-pilgrimage/routes-to-santiago/the-routes-today/the-paris-route
http://culture-routes.net/routes/the-saint-martin-of-tours-route

CAMINHO PORTUGUÊS

http://www.csj.org.uk/planning-your-pilgrimage/routes-to-santiago/the-route-in-portugal
http://caminoways.com/ways/portuguese-coastal-way-caminho-da-costa
https://portugal.com/portugal/cities/fatima

ITALY

http://www.csj.org.uk/via-francigena

ENGLAND

http://britishpilgrimage.org/where/great-routes
http://www.csj.org.uk

RUSSIA

http://www.pravoslavie.ru/english/62358.htm
https://sacredsites.com/europe/russia/sacred_sites_of_russia.html
http://www.hermitary.com/articles/pilgrim.html

EASTERN EUROPE

http://www.medjugorje.org/medinfo.htm
http://www.romania-insider.com/religious-romania-churches-and-monasteries-that-attract-the-largest-crowds-of-pilgrims-every-year
http://www.viasanctimartini.eu/walking-tours/saint-martin-pilgrimage-route
http://www.caminogalicja.pl/malopolskadroga_en.html

Camino Ways App: Retrieved from http://caminoways.com/travel-tips/download-free-app

Thank You

I would like to thank all the people along the way who invited me into their mosques, temples and churches with welcoming arms. As for this book, it has been a lifelong journey of discovery.

Thanks to Madhavi Mackey for compiling the research and editing this book, and Chris Harris, the editor.

Thank you also to everyone I have met along the way. As always, any errors and omissions that may remain are mine.

God Bless.